CAMBRIDGE FIRST CERTIFICATE
Series Editor: Sue O'Connell

GW00732952

CAMBRIDGE FIRST CERTIFICATE
Listening and Speaking

NEW EDITION

Sue O'Connell with Louise Hashemi

Teacher's Book

CAMBRIDGE
UNIVERSITY PRESS

PUBLISHED BY THE PRESS SYNDICATE OF THE UNIVERSITY OF CAMBRIDGE
The Pitt Building, Trumpington Street, Cambridge, United Kingdom

CAMBRIDGE UNIVERSITY PRESS
The Edinburgh Building, Cambridge CB2 2RU, UK
40 West 20th Street, New York, NY 10011–4211, USA
477 Williamstown Road, Port Melbourne, VIC 3207, Australia
Ruiz de Alarcón 13, 28014 Madrid, Spain
Dock House, The Waterfront, Cape Town 8001, South Africa
http://www.cup.org

First published 1992
Second edition 2000
Reprinted 2001

Printed in the United Kingdom at the University Press, Cambridge

Typeface Sabon   *System* QuarkXPress (Apple Macintosh)

ISBN 0 521 66808 5 Student's Book
ISBN 0 521 77983 9 Teacher's Book
ISBN 0 521 77982 0 Set of 2 cassettes

Contents

Introduction

Who is this book for?

Cambridge First Certificate Listening and Speaking is for learners who need additional practice in listening and speaking skills in preparation for Papers 4 and 5 of the Cambridge First Certificate examination. It aims to provide motivating communicative practice in these skills along with effective exam training. Because it addresses more than examination skills, it is also suitable for non-exam learners at upper-intermediate level who want to develop their listening and speaking skills generally.

How is it organised?

The Student's Book is organised into eighteen units: eight listening units alternating with eight speaking units, and two exam style practice tests at the end of the book. Each unit introduces and practises particular aspects of a skill and deals with vocabulary items, language points or pronunciation features which are relevant to the topic and the type of communication. Learners then apply the knowledge gained in the first part of the unit to an exam format task.

The book begins with a Foundation unit which is designed to increase learners' awareness of key aspects of the listening and speaking skills and to help them to begin assessing their own performance in these skills. In this way, learners are encouraged to become actively involved in the learning process from the outset.

Each unit begins with a summary box to show students exactly which listening and/or speaking skills, which language, vocabulary or pronunciation point, and which exam skills will be covered. Each unit contains one or two Exam Tips which summarise key techniques to remember in connection with the specific question types.

The Teacher's Book contains a timing guide for each unit, detailed teaching notes, a key to the exercises and the tapescript.

How should the material be used?

The material is intended to be used in sequence because skills and exam techniques are built up gradually and there is an element of revision and recycling incorporated into the structure of the book. Speaking tasks, for example, often provide practice in using language which has been introduced in previous listening units.

Each unit provides between 60 and 80 minutes' work. There is scope for flexibility, however, and the Teacher's Book suggests ways of extending or reducing the teaching time needed.

Foundation unit Introduction

The purpose of the Foundation unit is:

- to increase students' awareness of key aspects of the listening and speaking skills.
- to encourage students to think about their own performance in these skills and to begin analysing their strengths and weaknesses.
- to introduce some of the exam requirements for Papers 4 and 5.
- to explore students' preoccupations with regard to preparation for these papers.
- to introduce aspects of the syllabus and to reflect the methodology of the course, particularly in terms of student-centred work.
- to interest and motivate students at the start of the course.

What underlies these aims is the belief that learners are more likely to learn effectively if they are actively involved in the learning process from the outset and if learning is a collaboration between teacher and student.

My own experience as a teacher over the years has suggested that part, perhaps a large part, of the benefit of a teaching approach can be lost to students when they don't understand why they are asked to do certain things in certain ways. Students come with their own expectations of a course and may be bewildered if these aren't met. Pairwork and groupwork activities, for example, are a novelty to some and may, unbeknownst to the teacher, be very unpopular. It's all too rare for students to have the opportunity to discuss their reactions to the course with their teacher.

The Foundation unit therefore sets out to establish a dialogue between learners and teacher on the subject of the learning process. Without this, much of the benefit of the learner training element in the book may be lost, and many of the teaching and learning strategies may be misunderstood or resisted.

For this reason, answers are limited to facts (mark schemes, stress, pronunciation), while questions of interpretation and learning styles are deliberately left open. This is the time for discussion and 'seed sowing' rather than prescriptive statements.

Foundation unit

Timing guide

80–90 mins (Listening: 55–60;   Speaking: 25–30)

Note: This unit can be used in a number of ways, to fit your teaching timetable. The two parts can be done together or in two separate sessions. If you haven't time to cover all the material, however, you could reserve certain sections, and integrate them in later lessons.

Listening

Exercises 1 and 2 are intended to provide gentle awareness-raising and to encourage predictive listening.

1 Monitor students while they are working and encourage them to think of the correct term for each speaker, if possible, and any other relevant vocabulary. Ask them to suggest what the speaker might actually be saying in each case.

Teach relevant vocabulary (e.g. *platform, loudspeaker* **E**; *lawnmower* **G**)

KEY   Listening

1 A presenter or newscaster; the news; general interest in world events

B (tourist) guide; the history of the building; general interest

C booking clerk in a theatre box office; details of the tickets available and their prices; information needed to book a ticket

D driving instructor; advice about driving technique or instructions about driving; practical information about what to do and where to go next

E station official; information about train arrivals and departures; practical information about train times and platform numbers

F actors; performing a play; entertainment

G next door neighbours; gardening, the weather, local gossip; friendly interest

H weather forecaster; weather prospects; practical information about a particular area

I teacher/lecturer; mathematics; information for study

---

2 Ask students to say which words helped them to do the exercise and check these.

   1 Picture D; *signal* (not *sign*); *pull over* (move closer to the side of the road). You could also teach *pull in* (move to the side of the road in order to stop), *pull out* (move out into the road) and *pull up* (slow down and stop).

   2 Picture E: Ask students to express this information as simply as possible (e.g. We're sorry that the train to Bedford is late).

   3 Picture C: Explain the three main levels of a theatre in Britain – *stalls, circle, gallery*.

   4 Picture H: Check *patchy* (not evenly spread but appearing in certain areas), *isolated* (single examples, not part of a general pattern) and *shower* (a short period of light rain).

Check that students don't identify their sentences by headings or letters. When they've finished, swap examples around and get other students to write the letters which they think match the sentences. You could also ask them to see if they can spot any mistakes.

KEY Listening

2 1 **D**   2 **E**   3 **C**   4 **H**

---

3 Do the first question with students as an example. The obvious answer is D but there could be reasons for giving other answers too, depending on the situation. Encourage students to express a personal opinion and emphasise that there are few hard and fast rules. Here, as elsewhere, the point is to get students thinking about the target skill analytically.

KEY Listening

3 1 D   2 B, F   3 E, H   4 A, F, I   5 C (e.g. cheque) I
6 D, E, H (e.g. finding an umbrella or taking the washing off the line)   7 A, B, E, (H)   8 G (you have the opportunity to ask questions)   9 E (the sound quality can be a problem)
Note: 8 and 9 are very much personal matters but still interesting to discuss.

---

4 Let students work together to do this matching task quickly. Stop the tape briefly after each extract to allow students to write answers. Play a second time for checking and discussion.

KEY   Listening

4 Instructions **D**   Weather forecast **H**
Short talk **B**   Lecture **I**
Conversation between friends **G**   News bulletin **A**
Telephone conversation **C**   Joke **G**?
Film or play **F**   Public announcement **E**

1 Recorded message
2 Radio documentary
3 Traffic report
4 Advertisement
5 Conversation between friends
6 Directions

Tapescript

4 1 Hello, it's Erica. I'll ring you back at about four. By-ee.

2 Man 1:   ... Cooper's recent work was:

   Woman: 'Women in almost all jobs were less stressed and coped better than their male colleagues.'

   Man 1:   Quote.

   Man 2:   'In fact, I can't think of a job where women don't cope better than men, except, perhaps, those where they're still breaking the mould, like a female barrister in an all-male Chambers or a woman miner or fire-fighter.'

3 Good news in the City of Bristol. I've been told that Colston Street is now open. If you remember, it was closed earlier on with bits of the Colston Hall falling into the footway. It is now open. If you use the Gloucester Road as your home-going commuter route – I see lots of you outside the control room endeavouring to get home – the news is not good...

4 It's in colour with superb action pictures and is bigger and better than ever. Yes, the Evening News celebrates City's FA Cup tie with Cambridge United at Branston Gate tonight by publishing a magnificent 20-page special edition. On sale at newsagents and at the ground.

5 A: I've never understood what people get out of climbing – because it's... (*It seems to me just the same thing...*) well...I do admire the people who do it but somehow or other it's something that just doesn't appeal to me, but I suppose it is a similar kind of thing though...

   B: But that's a personal view. I think it's exactly similar in that you're competing with some natural...some natural force, really.

   A: I agree, I agree absolutely. There's some real kind of...physical, I suppose you'd say physical danger. (*Oh, yes.*)

6 I know where that is. Umm…you've got a little way to go, I'm afraid, and you're going to have to turn round. Umm…it is, in fact, about half a mile away, so you have to turn round, go back the way you came and follow the road right down to the T-junction…

First Certificate listening

Most students have some idea of what to expect in the exam but it is helpful to confirm what the main FCE Paper 4 question types are, and to correct any misapprehensions at this stage. Discuss the different question types briefly – find out what students like and dislike, find easy and difficult, and what they feel they need practice in.

KEY   First Certificate listening

1 The only unlikely types of listening are the film or play, the joke, the part of a novel and the poem.

2 Old-fashioned dictation passages do not occur in FCE.
You won't be asked to take free notes.
You won't be asked to draw or label a diagram.
You won't be asked to tick any answers.
All the answers, except in Part 2, consist of a single letter (A, B, C, or T, F etc.). In Part 2, you have to write down short answers (never more than a few words, and never whole sentences).
You write your answers on the question paper. At the end of the test, you have five minutes to copy your answers onto the special answer sheet.

Speaking

What does the First Certificate Speaking test consist of?

This is a basic description of the procedure for the First Certificate Speaking test and an opportunity to answer any questions students may have at this stage. It's worth emphasising that the test is always taken by candidates in pairs*, and that pair practice in class is therefore very important. It's also a good idea to explain that one of the examiners is there to conduct the test, and will talk to the candidates, explaining what they have to do, while the other concentrates on assessing their performance, and therefore does not join in the conversation at all.

The whole aim of the Speaking test is to find out how well the candidates can speak English, not how well they can describe a photograph or solve a problem! The test tasks are designed to do just that. Each of the four parts of the test is designed to offer candidates the opportunity to use different types of language: talking about themselves, making comparisons and contrasts, communicating interactively and discussing ideas and giving opinions. The four-part format of the test is fairly rigid, and each part is discussed separately as the different activities arise during this book.

(*Where there are an odd number of candidates, the last three take the test together.)

KEY   What does the First Certificate Speaking test consist of?

1 part   2 other   3 but / (al)though   4 on   5 with
6 points / parts / aspects   7 solve / discuss

Preparing for the Speaking test

1 This is a useful chance to find out about students' preconceptions. It's important to accept that all items are potentially useful but that because people's learning styles differ, particular items may be more useful to some people than to the others.

Discuss, in particular, the limitations of certain items (e.g. studying grammar rules, doing written grammar exercises or reading dialogues in a textbook) and the potential benefits of others which students may not be aware of (e.g. playing games in English in class). Highlight the self-help techniques that students can use.

2 This is a trick question, in a way, since all four areas have equal weighting in the exam. It is important to stress the importance of communication, discourse management and pronunciation, making sure that students understand what is meant by them, and to relate them to the activities in question 1 above. In addition to the four marks given by the assessor for these areas, there is a fifth, global, mark which is given by the interlocutor. This is based on a combination of the four areas and takes overall task achievement into account as well.

KEY   Preparing for the Speaking test

All four areas are equally important.

Pronunciation check

1 This is an initial sensitisation exercise which students may find quite difficult to begin with. If this is so, reassure them that they will improve quickly with practice. It will help, too, if you build in some regular extra word and sentence stress practice as you go through the course.

Spend some time practising the four examples before setting the task. When you play the tape, you may find it helpful to stop and replay each item to build up students' confidence in identifying stress.

2 Again this is an initial introduction to sounds and phonemic symbols. If students haven't come across the symbols before, it's worth pointing out the benefits of understanding them when they are used in dictionaries and coursebooks.

You could begin by illustrating the problem of spelling versus pronunciation in English: write the words *cough, tough, though, bough* on the board (there are also *thorough* and *hiccough*!). How would they know how to pronounce these words?

Elicit the sounds represented by the four phonemic symbols introduced here, starting with /e/, and spend some time clarifying and practising them, letting students watch and imitate the shape of your lips and so on.

Some students will find the task easier than others to start with. Let them compare their lists and help each other before playing the tape and checking answers.

KEY   Pronunciation check

1 apólogise   télephone   fórecast   documéntary
compáre   advértisement   vocábulary   repórt
nécessary   díctionary   conversátion   ínterview

2 *Group 1*   funny   rough   wonder   enough   son
Group 2   long   gone   shock   cough   wander
Group 3   key   week   peace   niece   ceiling
Group 4   health   head   said   left   meant

Tapescript

1 apologise   telephone   forecast   documentary
compare   advertisement   vocabulary   report
necessary   dictionary   conversation   interview

2 *Group 1*   funny   rough   wonder   enough   son
Group 2   long   gone   shock   cough   wander
Group 3   key   week   peace   niece   ceiling
Group 4   health   head   said   left   meant

Communication

This should be a fun final activity. Again, let students compare answers before you play the tape. It's useful practice for them to repeat after each exchange on the tape. Draw their attention to general intonation features here, encouraging them to exaggerate a little if possible.

When you are checking the types of communication, ask for further examples of each one, if there's time.

KEY Communication

1 f   2 e   3 h   4 c   5 i   6 b   7 a   8 d   9 g

apologising (8);   asking for directions (2);   giving an opinion (7); expressing gratitude (9);   giving advice (6);   greeting casually (4); meeting (for the first time) (1);   offering help (5);   requesting permission (3).

Tapescript

1 A: How do you do?
   B: How do you do?

2 A: I'm looking for King Street.
   B: It's second on the left.

3 A: Would you mind if I opened the window?
   B: No, not at all.

4 A: Hi! How are you?
   B: Fine thanks.

5 A: Let me give you a hand.
   B: That's kind of you.

6 A: I'd take a taxi if I were you.
   B: Would you?

7 A: It's the craziest idea I've ever heard.
   B: Do you really think so?

8 A: I'm sorry to keep you waiting.
   B: Don't worry. It doesn't matter.

9 A: Thanks for all your help.
   B: That's OK. Don't mention it.

Unit 1 Time out

Timing guide

65–70 mins (Pre-listening: 15–20;   Listening practice 1: 5;
Listening practice 2: 10;   Language practice: 15–20;
Exam listening: 20)

Revision

You may like to start with a five-minute revision test of vocabulary from
the Foundation unit (e.g. newscaster, driving instructor, loudspeaker,
signal/indicate, lawnmower, pull over/up/out).

Pre-listening

Note: This is an enjoyable activity which will take a minimum of 15
minutes. It can also easily 'expand' to fill 25 minutes, so if you only
have an hour at your disposal, don't allow too much discussion.

1 Give students one or two minutes to study the drawings on their own
and to identify the ones they don't know the English name for. Then
ask them to work with another student and see if they can find the
words they need. Try to avoid answering students' questions about
vocabulary at this stage. They should ask around to see if any other
student can help.

Go through the words and associated activities and check spelling as
necessary.

2 Inject some urgency into this by saying that students each have sixty
seconds to describe their leisure activity. It may also help to stop them
after about a minute and tell them to reverse roles.

Make sure to ask students to report back on what their partners have
said. This will encourage active listening in future pairwork activities.
If the class is large, ask a representative sample only.

KEY   Pre-listening

A   tennis racket (or racquet)
B   butterfly net
C   fishing rod
D   sailing boat / yacht / dinghy
E   compass; mountain climbing, orienteering etc.

F hockey stick
G golf club
H goggles (or mask); motorcycling, skiing, snorkelling etc.
I walking boots; trekking, climbing etc.
J telescope; astronomy etc.
K guitar
L saddle; (horse) riding
M ping pong (or table tennis) bat
N skis
O rucksack (or backpack); trekking, climbing etc.
P camera; photography (*check pronunciation*)
Q ice skating boots (or ice skates)
R tent; camping

Listening practice 1

Though the recordings are authentic, the task is quite simple and students are unlikely to need to hear the tape a second time. The aim is to build confidence and it would be inappropriate, therefore, to ask detailed comprehension questions or to focus on unknown vocabulary at this stage.

KEY   Listening practice 1

1 photography   2 skiing   3 horse riding   4 bird watching
5 sailing

Tapescript

1 The first part is to go out of your house and choose a subject matter to photograph, and that could range from a still life of some kind to a moving object such as a racing car or a riot or some street scene. I like the feel of the equipment whilst I'm taking the photograph.

2 Well I think it's the most amazing sport because I, I, I first had a go about twenty-five years ago, and obviously the equipment has changed quite a lot in the time since and it's become a lot safer. Um, the scenery's absolutely superb and the, the air is, is wonderful, and the speed and the exhilaration. You sleep well after it. And it's, for me it's just the best sport.

3 I think there's something rather special about it as a hobby, or a sport, um, because with most hobbies you just rely on yourself and maybe some equipment. Um, but here, you're depending on an animal and quite a powerful animal at that. So you have to build up a special relationship of trust between you. And if you um, if you do build up that relationship of trust, and if you develop some skill, then there's enormous satisfaction and

pleasure in what you can do together, um whether it's walking quietly along a lane or galloping over open countryside.

4 One of the things I find most interesting is there are something like six and a half thousand different types of birds in the world, that's six and a half thousand species of birds, and it's only in the last fifty to a hundred years, perhaps, that people have started looking at birds as something beautiful to admire in their own setting. Prior to that, we ate birds. We still do. Birds were shot and killed for their feathers, to put in hats, to decorate clothes. Birds were used. Whereas now, a lot of people who enjoy looking at birds, simply do that.

5 You're using the force of the wind to get around over the earth's surface, as people did two thousand years ago. And it has been complicated – boats have become more complicated, and navigation equipment has become electronic and complicated. But these are luxuries, the essential skills are exactly the same as they were two thousand years ago. And I think that's the, the fun.

Listening practice 2

Check understanding of the task and emphasise the slightly different instructions for each part.

Ask students to suggest how they could help themselves with a question like this in the exam, in the time before they hear the recording. They will probably suggest reading through the list but this is an opportunity to point out the value of thinking about how the words are pronounced too (see Exam Tip 1). Ask students to read the list aloud and correct any errors.

1 It will probably not be necessary to replay the tape.

2 Students will probably appreciate a second hearing of the tape.

KEY   Listening practice 2

1 printing, negative, (photograph *not* photographic), dark room, enlarge, film, develop.
2 riding mac, gloves (short stick *not* shooting stick), (saddle only needed by someone buying a horse), hard hat, riding boots.

Tapescript

1 I enjoy photography principally because it's creative. There are three elements to that creativity. The first part is to go out of your house and choose a subject matter to photograph, and that could range from a still life of some kind to a moving object such as a racing car or a riot or some street scene. I like the feel of the, the equipment whilst I'm taking the

photograph. The second part is to bring the film home and, in the dark room, to develop the film. You never quite know what's going to come out. The third part is the printing of the picture itself from the negative. And, in each of those stages, uh, more importantly the first stage and the last stage, you do have quite a large element of creativity. And particularly in the last stage, because you have your subject matter and you, and you can make it lighter or darker, or you can exclude things in the picture that you don't like, or you can enlarge one part of it and make a picture out of just that part excluding the rest. And that's why it's so different from taking a, a film to a shop where you just have the negative printed as it appears and there's nothing really you can do with it. So the reason I like photography is because of its creativity.

2 Well, you don't need a lot of equipment, not at the beginning, at least. Um, the most important thing, I think, is, is a hard hat because that can save you from quite nasty injuries to your head. Um, the second thing that's important is proper riding boots, or at least boots with a proper heel, because again, they can prevent nasty accidents. You see ordinary boots can get stuck in the stirrups if you fall off, which you probably will do, and you can get dragged along by the horse then. After that, well, I suppose riding trousers are advisable because they're much more comfortable than jeans, say, and they prevent you from getting sore legs. Gloves are useful, too. If you decide to go on with riding and to take it up seriously, then you would need a proper riding jacket and maybe a riding mac – that's a raincoat for riding in wet weather. And a crop – that's a, a short stick. And if you actually decide to buy a horse, then there's no end to all the equipment you'll need! I mean a good saddle and bridle cost the earth these days and they're only the beginning…

Language practice

1 If you are short of time, this task can be set for homework. You could then get students to complete the reference section at the start of the following lesson.

If done in class, give students five minutes to tackle the task on their own and then a few minutes to compare answers.

2 You may, of course, want to add one or two more expressions here.

KEY   Language practice: Expressions of location

1 The missing words are: 1 along 2 on 3 hand 4 at 5 In
6 hand 7 On 8 opposite 9 on 10 across/along 11 in
12 hand 13 at 14 along 15 between 16 hand
The position of the taxi stand (T) and bus stop (B) are shown opposite.

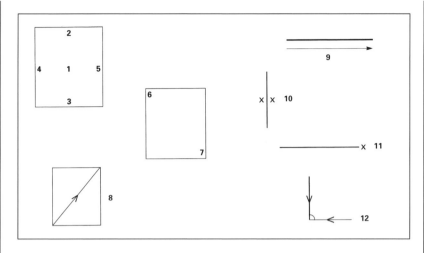

2 1 in the middle
   2 on the far side (at the top)
   3 half way along (at the bottom)
   4 on the left
   5 on the right
   6 in the top left hand corner
   7 in the bottom right hand corner
   8 across
   9 along
   10 on either side
   11 at the end
   12 at right angles

Exam listening

Let students work together to label the drawings and encourage them to practise saying the words (see Exam Tip 1). Check meanings and pronunciation, as necessary.

Make sure that they understand *warden* and *toddlers* before they listen.

1 After playing the tape the first time, allow students to compare answers.

2 Make sure students know what they have to do during the second playing and draw their attention to the advice in Exam Tip 1.

When they have answered the questions, play the tape again, pausing at the points where key information is mentioned (underlined in the tapescript).

3 Students might also work individually to draw sketch plans of the community centre and compare results. This is not an exam activity, but would be useful reinforcement of expressions of location and comparison.

KEY   Exam listening

1 The only items which aren't in the community centre are the cooker (which they hope to get), wheelchair (no access at present) and word processor (stolen).

2 1 T   2 F   3 T   4 F   5 T   6 T   7 F

Tapescript

A: Local teenagers have been in the news recently because they're trying to raise money for their youth club. So I've come here to <u>their base here at the community centre</u> in Moor Street to talk to Stacey Goodwin, who's the warden. First of all, Stacey, perhaps you'd like to show me round a bit?

B: Well, yes. This is the main hall where we're standing, by the front door, and it's quite big, you see, we've got a table tennis table out at the moment, and there's a volleyball net up for the girls under-fourteen team who'll be here this afternoon. And we have <u>other sports equipment too, which we keep in the big storage cupboard</u> over there on the right. If I could just show you …

A: Oh and lots of <u>things for younger children too, I see</u>.

B: Yes, we have plenty of <u>play equipment for the Mothers and Toddlers club</u> which is here three mornings a week.

A: So they're quite well provided for?

B: Yes, and in here, next to the storage cupboard, we have our little kitchen area, with a kettle and so on for making coffee and a sink to wash up afterwards. But <u>we can't cook anything, or even heat up food, which is one thing the youth club would like to do, so they want to have a cooker</u>, you know, and do burgers and stuff.

A: Right.

B: And then across the hall, we have a short corridor leading to the back door. The <u>room on the corner is for meetings</u>, you see, with table and chairs, it's <u>used by lots of small groups</u> in the community. Then next to that there's my office, just a desk and an old photocopier, really. I did have a word processor, but unfortunately it got stolen.

A: That's a problem, is it, security, I mean?

B: Oh, yes. And the kids raising money could really help about that because they want to change <u>the entrance area</u> so that people in wheelchairs could get in here …

A: Which they can't at present <u>with all those steps outside</u>.

B: Exactly. And new doors'd be much more secure.

A: Yes, of course. And here beyond the office you've got the ladies and gents, and on the wall opposite, I see <u>your notice board</u>.

B: <u>Actually, it's just there at the moment. It should be in the main hall</u> beside the door, but the hook's broken.

A: Maybe that's something else <u>the teenagers</u> can fix for you.

B: Yeah. Well, <u>they're working very hard</u> to improve the premises, so if you come back in six months, it should look quite a bit different.

A: I'll certainly look forward to doing that. And now here are some details of how listeners can help the youth club with their fund-raising efforts. This is where the youth club meets two evenings a week. …

Unit 2 **Every picture tells a story**

Timing guide

70–75 mins (Vocabulary: 20;   Pronunciation: 5;   Photographs: 10;
Language practice: 10–15;   Speaking test practice 1: 10;
Speaking test practice 2: 15)

Revision

If you have time, you could revise vocabulary related to leisure activities
or expressions of location from Unit 1.

Vocabulary

These tasks provide a review and extension of adjectives describing
mood and expression. If students are already familiar with most of
them, you could add some extra ones.

1 Let students carry out the exercise before you help with words they
don't know. Use the checking phase to check and clarify particular
items.

Make sure they understand the difference between *bored* and *boring*,
tired and *tiring*. You could include other pairs which are commonly
confused, e.g. *interested* and *interesting* and make a mini teaching
point of this if there's time.

The grouping of some words is very much a matter of personal
opinion so various answers could be acceptable, as long as students
show they understand the words and can explain their decisions.

2 It's useful to practise giving phrases like *terribly excited* and
absolutely furious appropriately dramatic intonation patterns, and to
contrast these with the milder *slightly nervous* or *quite contented*. If
students try reversing the patterns, using the dramatic intonation with
the mild statements and vice versa, it introduces an element of
humour and reinforces the importance of using appropriate
intonation.

KEY   Vocabulary

Various answers could be acceptable. Here is a possible grouping:

Positive   contented   amused   cheerful   interested   happy
thrilled   delighted

Negative	disappointed	bored	threatening	tired	disapproving
	worried	exhausted	furious	shocked	tiring
	annoyed	boring	anxious		
Neutral	serious	sleepy	nervous	excited	curious

Pronunciation 1: Word stress

Let students compare their answers and make any changes they want to before they listen to the tape. Stop the tape and replay each word if necessary.

KEY Pronunciation 1: Word stress

☐	☐	☐	☐
disappointed	excited	furious	contented
☐	☐	☐	☐
interested	cheerful	threatening	nervous
☐	☐	☐	☐
exhausted	disapproving	delighted	annoyed

Tapescript

disappointed	excited	furious	contented
interested	cheerful	threatening	nervous
exhausted	disapproving	delighted	annoyed

Photographs

Encourage the students to think of imaginative ideas and accept any well-argued and plausible suggestions. If you think students would like to know the real answers afterwards, here they are:

A Oscar Sherman Wyatt Junior, an oil millionaire from Texas on the day when his company was placed on the London Stock market.

B Spectators on a rainy day at Wimbledon.

C Children at a Christmas party. The caption reads 'Granny told us that one but it's still funny.'

D Teenage girls receiving exam results.

Tapescript

A He looks terribly tired. It looks as if he's at a meeting, a meeting that's been going on for a long time, I'd say. Maybe all day. It must be evening because the table lamp is on. He could be a politician or a businessman. He may be suffering from jet lag.

B   Let me see. Gosh, they look really fed up, don't they? Well, it must be raining because they've got their umbrellas up. It looks as if they're at some kind of sports event. They could be at a tennis match, maybe at Wimbledon. They might be waiting for the rain to stop and play to start. No wonder they're fed up!

C   They look very amused! It looks as if they've heard a good joke. They might be at a party. Yes, I think it must be a Christmas party because they're wearing paper hats and I think those are Christmas crackers in their hands.

D   Well, it's obviously not bad news. It could be exam results because it looks like an official sort of letter. They all look pleased about it, so I guess it's pretty important to them. They might have been worrying about them, and now they're feeling relieved.

Language practice

Draw students' attention to the grammatical features of each structure and ask them to suggest further examples.

Pronunciation 2: Sentence stress

1 You may like to introduce the subject of sentence stress with one or two easy examples:

(I'm pleased to meet you. He's working in a bank.

I'll see you on Saturday.)

Ask students to pick out the two main stresses in each sentence. Point out that the important words – the words which carry the meaning – are stressed. Ask what kind of words these would be (i.e. content words: nouns, verbs, adjectives). Students could then do the task in pairs.

2 Again, students could work together to help each other remember what was said and practise the expressions.

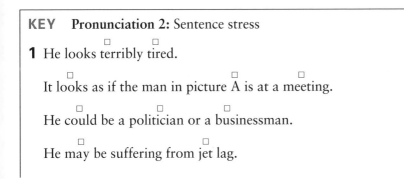

KEY   Pronunciation 2: Sentence stress

1 He looks terribly tired.

It looks as if the man in picture A is at a meeting.

He could be a politician or a businessman.

He may be suffering from jet lag.

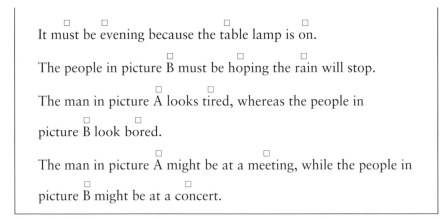

It must be evening because the table lamp is on.

The people in picture B must be hoping the rain will stop.

The man in picture A looks tired, whereas the people in

picture B look bored.

The man in picture A might be at a meeting, while the people in

picture B might be at a concert.

Tapescript

He looks terribly tired.
It looks as if the man in picture A is at a meeting.
He could be a politician or a businessman.
He may be suffering from jet lag.
It must be evening because the table lamp is on.
The people in picture B must be hoping the rain will stop.
The man in picture A looks tired, whereas the people in picture B look bored.
The man in picture A might be at a meeting, while the people in picture B might be at a concert.

Exam Tips

Optional pairwork activity: Each student reads one of the Exam Tips and pairs then exchange information. The discussion which is generated helps make the learning process more active.

Speaking test practice 1: Talking about a pair of pictures

Make sure students have read through the Exam Tip. Encourage them to give their opinions and to give reasons for them. Check that they are listening to their partners and agreeing or disagreeing appropriately.

Speaking test practice 2: Deciding which one you prefer

Again, make sure students have read through the Exam Tip. Encourage them to give reasons for their preferences.

Unit 3 Who, what, where?

Timing guide

65–75 mins (Pre-listening: 20;   Listening practice: 15;
Language practice: 20–25;   Exam listening: 10–15)

Revision

If you have time, you could start by revising some of the vocabulary for describing mood and expression from Unit 2.

Pre-listening

1 It is probably best to ask this question before students open their books so that they are not distracted by other items on the page.

You could ask students to discuss ideas in pairs though this would take longer. Offer one or two suggestions if students are short of ideas but it's better not to cover all the situations from the examples in question 2. Possible occasions are when:

– you're being introduced to somebody
– somebody is giving you directions
– you're listening to an announcement in a station or an airport
– you're taking a telephone message for somebody

2 This is a good exercise for pairwork. It's generally best to ask students to cover up the situations given at the bottom of the page initially. To help weaker students, or to speed up the activity, however, you could point out the choice of answers below at the outset. Tour round while students are working to make sure they are explaining the reasons for their decisions.

When checking answers, ask students to say which words helped them identify each situation.

3 It's helpful to suggest an answer for the first extract, as an example. Again, this works best as a pairwork activity.

KEY   Pre-listening

2 1 airport (boarding, Gate 6)   6 traffic report (blocked,
2 local news (got away etc.)   carriageway, junctions)
3 weather forecast (minus 2)   7 sports report (ridden, jockey)
4 telephone (number, redial)   8 railway station (boarding,
5 television (Channel 4)   platform)

3 Example answers
1 Flight number BA 037 to Moscow...   5 Next week's programme...
2 The robbers...   6 An accident...
3 Temperatures...   7 The race...
4 The number you are calling...   8 The Glasgow train...

Listening practice

These exercises give students practice in the useful basic listening skills
of scanning the specific information and identifying general context.
They should help to increase students' confidence since it's not necessary
for them to understand the details of each extract in order to perform
the tasks successfully.

KEY   Listening practice

1 1 c   2 d   3 b   4 e   5 a

2 1 j   2 c   3 a   4 d   5 f

3 1 7,000   2 £4.95   3 A394   4 40%   5 723779

4 1 a newscaster / radio or TV reporter   2 d actor
3 g radio announcer   4 f weather forecaster   5 e doctor

Tapescript

1 and **2**

1 Hello, John. I've just had a call from Gordon in the Washington office. He
needs the latest sales figures. Can you fax them to him right away?

2 Yes, I'd like to know the price of an air ticket to Toronto, please. First class.

3 Reports are coming in of an earthquake in a small town 50 miles north of
Sydney. Damage is said to be extensive. This is the first serious earthquake to
have hit Australia this century. We'll give you the details as they come in.

4 Come with us for the holiday of a lifetime. We'll take you to the land of the Pharaohs. You'll have two nights in Cairo with a chance to see the pyramids, and then a relaxing cruise on a luxurious Nile steamer. Call Darren on 530493 for details.

5 And now temperatures around the world: Athens is sunny and 10 degrees Celsius at the moment...

3 and 4

1 Police are to interview residents of the village where the missing businessman, Tom Greening, lived. This will mean interviewing up to 7,000 people.

2 London: the sights (*sound of Big Ben*) the shows (*wow!*), the shops (*sound of cash till*). Whether you visit on business or for pleasure, travel by Dart, the reliable route to the capital. At £4.95 return, it costs so little you can afford to make a day of it! Advance payment by Access or Visa, or pay the driver.

3 And on to the roads: in Oxford, on the A394, there are roadworks and temporary traffic lights. Long hold-ups can be expected. Obviously one to avoid there.

4 The weather check: staying cloudy tonight with a 40% chance of rain or drizzle. Tomorrow it's going to start dry with bright spells.

5 ...so take this prescription to the chemist and start taking the tablets straight away. And if you'd ring up towards the end of the week, we'll be able to give you the results of your X-rays. You've got the number? It's 723779.

Language practice

Telephone numbers

In British English, the first is normally pronounced:
three – seven – oh – double four (or four four) – six, extension two – nine – oh.
In American English, 0 is normally pronounced zero.

You could also practise stress which is used to divide up a number and make it more memorable, e.g. *three seven oh, double four six, or two nine, double seven, double six.*

Prepositions of time

These are revision exercises, intended to focus students' attention on language that can provide important listening clues (see Exam Tip 5). As such, they should be dealt with fairly quickly unless your students are weak in this area. In question 3, get students to cover the possible answers initially, and work through the text with them, asking for suggestions as to the type of time expression needed in each space.

If you have 10–15 minutes to spare, you could give students communicative practice in using time expressions by letting them do the diary information gap activity from Unit 4 (Speaking test practice 2, page 28).

Phrasal verbs

An optional activity which could be set for homework if time is short.

KEY   Language practice

Prepositions of time

1 in – parts of the day, months, seasons and years
at – exact moments of time
on – days and dates

2 by   – latest time an action will finish
for   – how long an action has been going on
from – starting point of an action in the past or future
since – when an action, which is still going on, started

3 1 Saturday 17th   6 a few days
2 8 pm   7 next weekend
3 the evenings   8 ages
4 a Saturday   9 your birthday
5 the second half of July

Phrasal verbs

1 put...through   5 rang up
2 hold on   6 call back
3 cut off   7 get through
4 hang up

Exam listening: Any messages?

Make sure students have time to read through the instructions and check that they are understood before beginning. It's also useful to reinforce the point made in Exam Tip 5 (this unit) again by asking them to predict the kind of information they are going to hear.

KEY Exam listening: Any messages?

Exercises 1 and 2

	FROM	SUBJECT	MESSAGE
1	Peter Harris	g	Please collect as soon as possible £65 **(1)** to pay. Phone 733748.
2	Sheila	d	Can you come on 30th **(2)** at 8 pm? Call (New York) 939 4557.
3	Mike Paxton	c	Could come round this evening. Phone 445010 **(3)** before 5.30 **(4)**.
4	Janet Wright	e	Change of date to Feb 15th **(5)** is this ok? Phone Oxford 791648 **(6)** extension 2321.
5	Colin	b	Suggest leaving at 7.10 **(7)** Have you got the tickets? **(8)** Phone 724601.
6	Emily	a	Thank you for **(9)** the record token. Going to get a tape of Scottish folksongs **(10)**.

Tapescript

1 This is Peter Harris on Redland 733748, I repeat, 733748. Your little rocking chair has been repaired and is now ready for you. The cost is £65, as we agreed. I'd be grateful if you could pick it up please because I haven't got a lot of storage space. Give us a ring, please. Bye.

2 Hi, surprise, surprise! It's Sheila here. I'm calling from New York. Got your card – many thanks. Look, I'm coming over for a flying visit next weekend. It's my parents' golden wedding anniversary so I'm arranging a little celebration with all their old friends as a surprise. It's on the 30th, about 8 o'clock. Would you like to come? They'd love to see you and so would I. Let me know if you can make it. Do you know my number? It's 939 4557 – New York – I'm not sure what the code from the UK is. Uh, speak to you soon, I hope.

3 Hello, this is Mike Paxton. Um. Sorry I couldn't get back to you any earlier. I'm phoning from Kingsdown. I'll be here till 5.30 – it's now, um, 3 o'clock. I have the spare part to repair your typewriter and I could fit it this evening if that's all right. So could you call me to say if that's OK? My number is 445010. Did you get that? 445010. Bye.

4   Good afternoon. It's Janet Wright, Mark Andrew's secretary. We're thinking of changing the date of the next committee meeting from February 22nd to Thursday February 15th. I'm just ringing to ask whether or not it would be convenient if we did change the date or whether you would have any objections. Perhaps when you've got a moment, you could give me a ring on Oxford 791648 Extension 2321. Thank you.

5   What a long time you have to wait for that beep! Uh this is Colin on 724601 – well you know that anyway! Erm, about tonight, I suggest we leave, if we want to walk to the theatre, about ten past seven, something like that. I don't think it's going to rain. Oh, ah one thing, um, I hope you've got the tickets because I don't seem to have them. And we'll be a bit stuck if they're lost! Give me a call when you get in. Bye.

6   Hello Aunty Sarah. This is Emily. Thank you for the token, um, the record token which you sent for my birthday. (*Tell Aunty Sarah what you're going to buy with it.*) I think I'll get a tape… (*You said you wanted a tape of folksongs, didn't you?*) yes, a tape of Scottish folksongs. (*Give her our love.*) Mummy and Daddy send their love. Bye.

Unit 4 It can't have been the octopus!

Timing guide

60–75 mins (Pronunciation 1: 5–10;   Quiz Part 1: 10;
Pronunciation 2: 10;   Quiz Part 2: 5–10;   Speaking test practice 1:
10–15;   Speaking test practice 2: 10;   Speaking test practice 3: 10)

Revision

If you have time, you could revise vocabulary (*carriageway*, *registration*, *jockey*, *digit*) or phrasal verbs from Unit 3.

Discussing opinions

Pronunciation 1: Intonation

Begin by discussing what intonation is (i.e. the 'music' of the language). Illustrate the two basic patterns by saying a few single words first as statements and then as questions, e.g. No!/No?, Three/Three? Yesterday/Yesterday? You could give a little preliminary practice by saying a number of short phrases and asking students to identify whether they have a rising or a falling tune.

e.g. It's four o'clock. (falling) What time is it? (falling) What time is it?! (surprised – rising) Shall we meet this evening? (rising) Where are you going? (falling) How are you? (falling) Are you leaving? (rising)

After students have listened to the tape and compared answers, ask them to repeat each sentence with the appropriate intonation patterns.

Help them to produce a clear falling tune with statements and questions beginning with question words, and a clear rising tune with the questions which invite yes/no answers. Help them, too, to distinguish between definite answers (e.g. *No, I don't agree. That's a good idea.*) and more tentative answers (e.g. *You could be right.*) which have a less strong falling.

KEY   Pronunciation 1: Intonation

1 What do you think? (falling)   Why do you say that? (falling)

Have you any idea…? (rising)   You could/may/might be right. (falling)

What's your opinion? (falling)   That's a good idea. (falling)

Are you sure? (rising)   No, I don't agree. (falling)

How do you know? (falling)   I'm not sure you're right. (falling)

2 Statements of fact generally have a falling tone.
Questions with question words generally have a falling tone.
Questions with yes/no answers generally have a rising tone.

Tapescript

What do you think?
Have you any idea what the answer is?
What's your opinion?
Are you sure?
How do you know?

Why do you say that?
You may be right.
That's a good idea.
No, I don't agree.
I'm not sure you're right.

General knowledge quiz: Part I

It may be useful to give students a little revision of the language of speculation from Unit 2 before they begin. If you have time, you could do this by using:

– ambiguous pictures from newspapers or magazines.
– advertisements from newspapers or magazines with the name of the product hidden.
– a video recording of a TV advertisement, stopped before the name of the product is revealed and perhaps with the sound turned down.

Circulate while students are working to see how well they are using the target language (although they don't need to use it all the time). Encourage them and help them with ideas if they seem to be struggling.

As an extension or homework activity, students could prepare their own general knowledge questions for use in a future lesson.

> **KEY**   General knowledge quiz: Part 1
>
> A 1 Greenland (Australia is usually regarded as a continental land mass rather than an island.)
>
> 2 The Nile and the Amazon. Some people claim the Nile is the longest and others claim that the Amazon is, depending on the definition of the word 'river' they use.
>
> 3 Canberra
>
> 4 The spinetail swift (a bird) of Asia has been timed at speeds up to 170 km/h (105.6 mph). The fastest of all land animals is the cheetah with a maximum speed of 101 km/h (63 mph).
>
> 5 The tortoise – the greatest age recorded is over 152 years.
>
> 6 The blue whale
>
> 7 The Siberian tiger
>
> 8 Moscow – it carries about 2 billion passengers a year. (The London Underground has the longest route in the world and the New York City Subway has more stations than any other underground system.)
>
> 9 Toronto – the CN (Canadian National) Tower (553 m) is the highest free-standing building in the world. The tallest office building is the Sears Tower in Chicago (443 m).
>
> 10 China – the China News Agency reported recently that there were 100 million TV sets with 600 million viewers in the country. (At the same time, the USA had approximately 90 million sets.)
>
> B   a) Austria   b) Canada   c) Switzerland   d) Ireland
>   e) Malta   f) Zambia

Language practice

It may be helpful to give students some initial practice in this target language, using verbal situations. For example:

– A lives in England. She arrived in Italy yesterday. How did she travel?
  She could've flown / travelled by train / taken a coach / hitch-hiked etc.

– B arrived in a new town. He needed a place to stay. What did he do?
  He might've asked a policeman / gone to Tourist Information / slept in the park etc.

– It takes 20 minutes to walk to the station. C left home five minutes before the train left and he caught the train. How did he do it?
  He must've taken a taxi / driven there by car; the train must've been late etc.

KEY   Language practice

1 a diary, address book or notebook which has been lost.
2 a shirt, blouse or jacket which has been wrongly returned at the cloakroom, dry cleaners or laundry.
3 some food which has made someone ill.

Tapescript

1 I must've lost it. I've looked everywhere! I might've dropped it on the bus, I suppose, or it might've fallen out of my bag when I was running for the bus. The trouble is, it's got lots of important numbers in it, which I haven't written down anywhere else. And people's birthdays and things. Oh God, I'd better ring the police station in case someone's handed it in.

2 So I took it back and showed it to the assistant 'This isn't mine,' I said. 'You must've given me the wrong one. You can't have checked the number on the ticket properly. It's the same colour but this is at least three sizes too big! And the one I brought in didn't have a mend on the sleeve.'

3 It must've been something I ate. It could've been the fish stew, I suppose. You said it had a funny smell at the time. It can't have been the octopus, though, because you had that too and you were all right.

Pronunciation 2: Sentence stress

You could spend a little time introducing students to the sound /ə/ in English (called 'schwa'). It's the sound we hear in the word *the* (e.g. the queen), and although it's never written, it's the most common vowel sound in the language. Write the following sentences on the board and ask students to say how many 'schwa' sounds there are in each.

– What's the time ? (1)
– It's a quarter past seven. (3)
– I'll be late for the lesson. (3)
– You'd better hurry. (1)

When students have done the first exercise, point out that /ə/ always occurs in unstressed syllables.

KEY   Pronunciation 2: Sentence stress

1 I must've lost it.

3 It must've been something I ate.

I might've dropped it.

It could've been the fish stew.

It could've fallen out of my bag.   It can't have been the octopus.

2 You must've given me the wrong one.

You can't have checked the ticket.

Tapescript

1 I must've lost it.
   I might've dropped it.
   It could've fallen out of my bag.
2 You must've given me the wrong one.
   You can't have checked the ticket.

3 It must've been something I ate.
   It could've been the fish stew.
   It can't have been the octopus.

General knowledge quiz: Part 2

This activity provides an opportunity to practise speculating about the past. Tour round to help students notice the clues in the names and to check how well they're using the target language.

KEY   General knowledge quiz: Part 2

Galileo	thermometer
Samuel F.B. Morse	single wire telegraph
Alfred Nobel	dynamite
Alessandro Volta	battery
Karl Benz and Gottlieb Daimler	motor car engine
Guglielmo Marconi	radio
King C. Gillette	safety razor
Wright Brothers	aeroplane
Ladislao Biro	ball point pen (the name Biro is a trademark in the UK and ball point pens are often called biros)
NASA	space shuttle

Speaking test practice 1

The exercise is designed to encourage students to talk about the visual clues and to discuss their ideas about the sequence of events that occurred. It should also elicit the target language *could've/must've/can't have* etc.

1 Give students time to read the instructions and to study the picture for a few minutes. Then ask them to discuss their answer to the first question (Who or what made the tracks marked A–D?) in pairs. Make sure they have agreed on the right answer (tell them, if necessary) before they go any further.

Tour round while they work to check that they have noticed all the details shown in the picture and that they are ready to give reasons for the conclusions they have come to.

2 This question is open to interpretation. Someone could have stolen it or they could have taken it somewhere for safe keeping.

3 If you are short of time (and your students are reasonably imaginative) you could ask the students to do this without turning to the role-play cues.

KEY Speaking test practice 1

1 A dog owner **B** dog **C** cat **D** cyclist

2 Someone was walking along with their dog when the dog saw a cat on the other side of the road. The dog dashed across the road in front of a cyclist who must have fallen off the bike as a result. The cat ran over a fence and climbed a tree to safety. The dog ran round the tree, trying to reach the cat, and then ran away (he could have run home). As soon as the accident happened, the dog owner ran to a nearby telephone box to call for an ambulance and then went to help the cyclist. Someone came out of the house opposite to see what had happened and then went back inside. When the ambulance arrived, the attendants helped the cyclist get in and then drove away. The dog owner must have travelled in the ambulance with the injured cyclist. Meanwhile somebody must have come from a field nearby, picked up the bicycle and wheeled it away. What might have happened to the bicycle?

Speaking test practice 2: Discussing advantages and disadvantages

This exercise encourages students to justify what they say. Remind them about Exam Tips 3 and 4. It also practises the use of superlatives. Monitor students' conversations carefully and note any errors or weaknesses that need attention.

Speaking test practice 3: Giving your personal opinion

Students should be encouraged to have fun and be inventive. Stress that *any* of the ways of travelling can be chosen, provided that it can be justified.

Unit 5 **Bear country**

Timing guide

60–70 mins (Pre-listening: 10–15;   Listening practice: 15;
Language practice: 15;   Exam listening: 20–25)

Revision

If you have time, you could start by revising *could be / might be /
must be / can't be* from Units 2 and 4, which will be useful for the
Pre-listening activity.

Pre-listening: Quiz

Note: A good introduction to the unit and to the topic is to give students
one or two minutes to write down any words they think of in
connection with Canada. These could be general words like *snow* or
mountains, names of cities, geographical features, animals, or words for
people e.g. *Eskimos (Inuit), mounties, lumberjacks*. Write the
suggestions up on the board and discuss briefly. (You could then cross
off any words which come up in the unit.)

The three parts of the quiz should take about ten minutes to do.
Encourage students to guess answers even if they say they don't know
anything about Canada. It's surprising, in fact, how many they can get
right after discussion with others in the class.

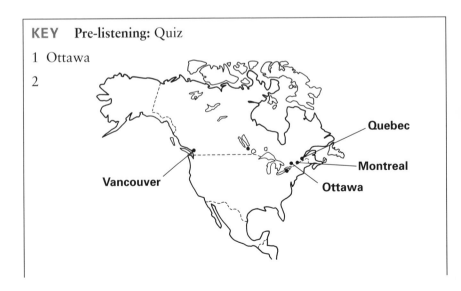

KEY   Pre-listening: Quiz

1 Ottawa

2

3 a) Alaska (the largest state of the USA)
  b) Lake Michigan (the third largest of the five Great Lakes and the only one completely in the USA)
  c) Seattle (the largest city in the state of Washington (USA) and the home of the Boeing Corporation)
  d) Long Island (island in New York State (USA) which contains the borough of Brooklyn and also Kennedy Airport)

Listening practice

You may need to help students with some vocabulary e.g. *waistcoat, salmon, whale* and *waffle* (a kind of thick pancake, as explained on the tape). It's unlikely that you will need to play the tape more than once.

KEY   Listening practice

1 second biggest	8 Quebec
2 26 million	9 Pacific salmon
3 forest	10 waffles
4 warm	11 foreign wine
5 an overcoat	12 woollen sweaters
6 quarter	13 dollar
7 Germans	

Tapescript

Thank you for calling the Daily News Information line on Canada.

Canada is a huge country, second in size only to the Soviet Union. Yet it has only 26 million people, which is less than half the population of the United Kingdom. It extends from the Great Lakes in the south to the majestic Rocky Mountains in the west, and the bleak Arctic Islands in the far north. A third of the country is covered by forest and there are also vast grasslands and countless lakes and rivers.

There are great variations in climate. Winters are extremely cold except in Vancouver which has a milder climate owing to its location on the west coast, so take a heavy overcoat and a fur hat. Canadian summers are warm on the whole, especially inland, so you'll only need lightweight clothing.

A quarter of all Canadians, mainly those living in the province of Quebec in the east, speak French as their first language. In addition, there are half a million American Indians, a million Germans and smaller numbers of Italians, Ukrainians and Inuit. Canada has two official languages: English and French, except in the province of Quebec where French alone is the official language. You'll find English spoken virtually everywhere apart from Quebec and if you plan to visit Quebec City, you'll definitely need a French phrasebook if you don't speak French.

Eating out is a pleasure in Canada and you'll find restaurants, coffee shops and snack bars to suit every pocket. Menus offer a wide choice with excellent seafood like Pacific salmon, lobsters and clams, meat dishes including moose steaks and beefsteaks, and also a range of ethnic foods. For the sweet course, the speciality is waffles, a kind of thick pancake, served with maple syrup. Beer is good but foreign wines, even those from neighbouring America, tend to be quite dear and local wines are not particularly good.

Canada has some of the world's most modern shopping centres. Clothes tend to be slightly expensive by European standards but there are some bargains to be had. Good buys include moccasins, a kind of soft leather shoe made by Indians, woollen gloves and sweaters, wood carvings, leather goods and maple syrup, of course.

The unit of currency is the Canadian dollar. Banking hours are from 10 am to 3 pm Monday to Thursday and till later on Fridays.

Have a good trip, and thank you for calling the Information line.

Language practice: Alternative words

You could ask students to close their books at this point and introduce the topic orally by writing the two extracts from the tape on the board and eliciting alternative ways of expressing the same meaning.

2 Some of these words are from the previous listening text and some preview the Exam listening text. Clarify meanings if necessary.

3 Help students if necessary by giving a mini context for each phrase. e.g.
Vancouver has a milder climate, *owing* to its location on the west coast.
Canadian summers are warm *on the whole*…
In addition, there are half a million Indians…
Wine *tends to be* quite dear…

KEY Language practice: Alternative words

1 are French speaking
Good things to buy are…

2
dear/expensive	enormous/huge
broad/wide	fasten/tie up
stretch/extend	miserable/unhappy
risky/dangerous	close/near
dessert/sweet	upright/erect
swift/fast	shot/photograph

3 because of, due to, as a result of
In general
furthermore, moreover, besides, also
'X' is usually

Exam listening

It's important to follow up the good habits encouraged in the Listening practice exercise and pointed out in Exam Tips. Ask students to guess how tall a grizzly bear would be when standing up, for example. It may be helpful to read through the right-hand side of the table with students and let them make suggestions at each gap. Don't accept or reject any specific suggestion at this stage, of course.

KEY Exam listening

A Know your bears

1	slopes	6	150
2	275	7	day
3	eyesight	8	680
4	smell	9	extreme north
5	camping	10	swim

B Camping safety

1	mosquitoes	6	shot/photo(graph)
2	your tent	7	get/come between
3	a bag	8	make a noise
4	over/from a tree	9	surprise
5	attack	10	bell

Tapescript

A   With so much land, Canada has a rich variety of wild animals, and if you go camping or hiking, you should be able to see a number of them. The largest and most dangerous animals you might meet in Canada are bears.

There are three main types:

The grizzly bear is the one you may have heard about. This bear is found on the higher slopes of the Rocky and Selkirk Mountains in British Columbia, Alberta and the Yukon. The grizzly is a very big animal and can be up to 275 cm tall when standing upright. Quite a terrifying sight, I can assure you. It has very poor eyesight but makes up for that with an excellent sense of smell and of hearing. To make matters worse, it's a very fast animal. The only good thing about the grizzly is that it can't climb trees. Like most bears, it's usually afraid of people but the grizzly is unpredictable and easily angered, so be warned.

The black bear is found in all regions of Canada and it's the one you have the best chance of seeing. It often wanders around camping grounds, cabins and garbage dumps looking for a snack. It's quite a bit smaller than the grizzly, usually less than 150 cm from nose to tail and weighing 90 kg. It's active during the day and unfortunately, it can climb trees.

The polar bear is also very large, up to 680 kg in weight, in fact, and has thick yellowish-white fur. It can only be found in the extreme north where, because of danger from hunting, it's a protected species. The polar bear moves quickly on land and can also swim long distances between coasts and icefloes.

B   If you go camping in the woods, you may be troubled by blackflies or mosquitoes. Remember to take a spray with you because these insects can make your life pretty miserable.

Another problem is the animals, most importantly bears, who are always looking for an easy meal. For this reason, don't leave scraps of food around the site and never, ever, keep your food in your tent or you may find you have an unwelcome visitor. Put any food in a bag, tie the bag to a rope and hang it over a tree away from your tent. Pull it up high enough so that a standing bear can't reach it.

Don't approach a bear too closely or it may get angry and attack. Take photographs, by all means, but don't be tempted to try to get a close-up shot of a bear – it's far too risky. And never get between a bear and its cubs.

A final point of advice: it's a very good idea to make a noise when you're walking through the woods or in the mountains in bear country. That way you won't surprise any bears. You can talk or sing as you go, or you may prefer to use a bell to announce your presence.

Unit 6 Pet hates

Timing guide

60–75 mins (Photo: 5–10;   Vocabulary 1 and 2: 15;   Language practice: 10–15;   Pronunciation: 10; Speaking test practice 1: 10; Speaking test practice 2: 10)

Revision

If you have time, you could revise vocabulary from Unit 5: some of the alternative expressions, for example, or specific items (e.g. *waistcoat, whale, salmon, cubs*) which were new to students.

Discussing a photograph

These tasks provide an opportunity to practise for the first part of the First Certificate Interview, the picture conversation. They allow students to describe and speculate about a photograph and also to use their imaginations freely in interpreting the visual evidence (see Exam Tip 4, Unit 2).

1 Monitor students as they work to check whether they are using some of the expressions they've learnt to speculate about what's happening.

2 Again, monitor and encourage students to be creative in their interpretations. Invite a few pairs (including the most imaginative) to explain their story.

Vocabulary 1

Students often let themselves down in the exam by using a much more limited vocabulary range than they are really capable of, so this is an important point which will need frequent reinforcement.

When checking answers, correct and practise pronunciation as necessary.

Optional extra practice activity: Students work in pairs to ask and answer questions using the adjectives in the exercise, as in the examples below:

A: Was it a big dog?
B: Big? It was absolutely huge!
A: Are you pleased about the news?
B: Pleased? I'm absolutely delighted!

This is a useful drill-type activity which practises vocabulary and pronunciation. It's helpful to give a demonstration using the first example with a student as A, and then the second example with a student as B. Practise the response in these examples, encouraging the students to use really expressive stress and intonation.

Make sure students can think of suitable questions (not only about animals!) and remind them that *absolutely* can only be used with extreme adjectives (it's not appropriate with *miserable* here).

KEY Vocabulary 1

big	huge/enormous	interesting	fascinating
small	tiny	tired	exhausted
old	ancient	angry	furious
frightened	terrified	hungry	starving
pleased	delighted	surprised	astonished/amazed
unhappy	miserable	silly	ridiculous

Vocabulary 2

1 Play the tape a second time if necessary. When checking, ask students which clues helped them to decide the answers.

2 Check answers after each section and replay, stopping the tape, if students find the task difficult. Clarify the meaning of new vocabulary.

KEY Vocabulary 2

1 1 kittens/cats 2 snakes 3 camels 4 spiders

2 *Group A* sweet playful affectionate clean fascinating beautiful (harmless)

  Group B revolting slimy nasty bad-tempered unpredictable vicious smelly horrible

---

Tapescript

1 Well, they were really sweet little things – very playful and affectionate. I didn't mind looking after them at all. They used to play for hours with their toy mouse or just curl up and go to sleep in their basket. They were no trouble, no, and they're very clean animals too.

2 I know it's a bit unusual but I really like them. I have done ever since I saw them in the zoo, as a child. I don't know why. Most people think they're revolting. They imagine that they're slimy to touch or something but that's not true – they're quite dry. I'm not saying they'd make a good pet or anything, and I wouldn't want to get too close to one of the poisonous ones, but I think the way they move is fascinating. Some of them have colours and patterns which are really beautiful.

3 Nasty, bad-tempered animals. We used them to carry equipment on the expedition and sometimes for riding as well. The worst thing is that they're so unpredictable. One moment they're behaving OK, the next they can be quite vicious. Mine used to try and grab my leg in his teeth every time I tried to get on his back – you get on while they're lying down, you know. The other problem is that they're really smelly. They have terrible breath! No, I'm not very fond of them at all.

4 It was absolutely huge. Honestly! It was in the bath for a few days and I had to get a friend to get rid of it in the end. I couldn't bear to go near it. I know they're harmless but I absolutely loathe them. I can't help it. Perhaps it's their colour or the way they move. Anyway, I think they're horrible.

Language practice: Expressing likes, dislikes and preferences

1 The aim here again is to encourage students to use a variety of expressions with really appropriate stress and intonation. If you are short of time, keep this brief and omit the tape practice.

2 Make sure students understand they should fill in the table for their partner. Monitor their work to see how varied their language is and how expressive their stress and intonation. Encourage them to keep up a fairly brisk pace so that the activity doesn't drag.

3 Include brief feedback from students here.

Tapescript

A: How do you feel about cats?
B: I really love them.

A: Do you like snakes?
B: I don't mind them.

A: How about camels?
B: I'm not very fond of them.

A: What are your feelings about spiders?
B: I absolutely loathe them!

B: I prefer cats to dogs, myself.
   I'd rather see an animal in the wild than in the zoo.

Pronunciation

Give students clear models of the four sounds and encourage them to listen carefully and to watch the shape of your mouth as you make the sounds. Make sure they can pronounce the sounds correctly themselves. Let them repeat the sounds after the tape for further practice. Explain meanings briefly, if necessary.

KEY   Pronunciation

Group 1   cat   salmon   rabbit   lamb
Group 2   shark   calf   carp   lark
Group 3   bear   mare   hare   lair
Group 4   worm   bird   herd   turkey

Tapescript

Group 1   cat   salmon   rabbit   lamb
Group 2   shark   calf   carp   lark
Group 3   bear   mare   hare   lair
Group 4   worm   bird   herd   turkey

Speaking test practice 1: Compare and contrast

Refer students to the exercises in Units 2 and 4 which also covered this part of the Speaking test. Remind them that it is important to support the opinions they offer, and encourage them to ask each other to do so.

Speaking test practice 2: Discussion

Check instructions and remind students that the aim is to express personal views and to discuss all the options thoroughly before reaching a decision. They should keep the conversation going even if they happen to agree at once! (If you think this is likely to happen, you could stipulate that one in each pair likes animals a lot while the other doesn't.) At the same time they should be prepared to be flexible if there are differences of opinion.

Monitor the conversations to make sure students are making the most of the material and using a good variety of language.

Unit 7 **All in a day's work**

Timing guide

70–75 mins (Pre-listening: 15–20; Listening practice 1: 10;
Language practice 2: 15; Listening practice 3: 10;
Listening practice 4: 10; Exam listening: 15)

Revision

If you have time, you could revise vocabulary from Unit 6 (animals and adjectives).

Pre-listening

It's a good idea to introduce the topic before students open their books. A simple idea would be to ask students to suggest ways in which someone could change their appearance (introduce the word *disguise*) and then ask them to think of jobs where it would be necessary to wear disguises.

The two activities are intended to be light-hearted but they also teach and revise a range of vocabulary to do with clothing.

1 As students work, tour round and encourage them to be as precise as possible in their descriptions. In other words, it's not enough to say *collar*. They must specify *behind* or *under the collar*. *Lapel* is a suitable alternative (with a slightly different meaning) and worth teaching when you go through the answers, if students don't know it.

2 Again, there is an opportunity to extend students' vocabulary at the checking stage.

KEY   Pre-listening

1 1 inside his hat band
2 pinned behind his collar/lapel
3 between the straps of his camera
4 inside the pen in his breast pocket
5 inside his cuff
6 under the (sticking) plaster on his hand
7 inside his sock
8 either under a false sole or inside his heel

2
1 The top of his hat is rounded rather than flat.
2 He's wearing sunglasses.
3 He hasn't got a moustache. (He's clean-shaven.)
4 His camera has a flash.
5 His belt is shorter.
6 He's wearing a ring on his right hand.
7 There isn't a right-hand breast pocket in his coat (and no pen).
8 There's one button fewer on his coat.
9 There's a tear in his coat. (His coat is torn.)
10 His trousers are plain rather than striped.

Listening practice 1

As a first stage, ask students to work in pairs and describe the pictures to each other. Ask them to look particularly for the small differences between the pictures. This follows the procedure recommended in Exam Tip 11 and will help students listen more effectively. Reassure students that here and in the other Listening practice exercises they can hear the tape a second time if necessary.

When checking, it may be useful to revise *done up / undone* and *do up / undo* for buttons, zips, belts, coats, jackets etc.

KEY Listening practice 1

D

Tapescript

Let's make no mistake, we are dealing with a very dangerous man. He'll stop at nothing to get the information he wants. And he's not going to be easy to catch. He's a master of disguise – we've had reports of him dressed in black leather and riding a motorbike, looking like a very old man and even posing as a ski instructor. He's been seen in town in the last couple of weeks and the latest reports tell us he's likely to be wearing a heavy overcoat with wide lapels and a collar which he often has turned up, even in fine weather. Another give-away is the dark glasses he always wears. He never seems to be carrying anything like a briefcase or a newspaper and he keeps his hands buried in his pockets. He may be carrying a gun, in fact, so be warned. Another thing, he's never been seen without a hat – it's an old fashioned one, a light colour with a dark hat band – makes him look like a gangster! One last small thing, our agents have noticed that the bottom button on his coat is always undone. Maybe he has difficulty bending to do it up.

Listening practice 2

When checking, ask students to tell each stage of the story rather than describe the pictures. Elicit useful vocabulary like *dashed* and *identical*.

KEY Listening practice 2

2 The correct order is: 1 5 4
                            6 3 2

3 Black Hat had noticed that the Master Spy was left-handed (see picture 6).

Tapescript

I knew there was only one place to find Z, the Palm Hotel, and I had to get there fast. I slipped a gun in my inside pocket. Z was a desperate man and when he found out I was on to him, he wasn't going to challenge me to a game of ping pong! Then I cycled to the Palm Hotel and waited in a doorway opposite. I didn't have to wait long. At about quarter past two, Z arrived by taxi and went into the hotel. I expected him to be wearing a disguise and I was right. But even with dark glasses and in a ridiculous green overcoat and cap, there was no mistaking Master Spy Z.

While he was checking in, I managed to make my way into the building. Hiding behind an old copy of *The Times*, I saw him enter the lift. As soon as the doors had closed, I dashed upstairs, two at a time, and arrived at the first floor landing just in time to see another man entering the lift. He was wearing a brown raincoat but I didn't see his face. I then raced up the stairs again, checking each floor to make sure the lift didn't stop, until I reached the top floor. When I got there, two men were leaving the lift. They were both dressed in brown raincoats and they looked identical but I knew one of them had to be Z. The problem was, which one? I followed the two men down the hall and watched as they took out their keys and let themselves into their rooms.

I wasn't in good shape. Those stairs had almost killed me! But I had spotted the clue I needed. Z couldn't fool me. I knew which room he was in and I was going to pay him a visit.

KEY Listening practice 3: Identifying the speaker

1 spy, actor, detective, motorcycle messenger, traffic warden, tourist guide

2 1 E   2 B   3 D   4 A   5 F

Tapescript

Speaker 1: I have to know my way round the city centre very well. I know all the places where people think they can get away with parking illegally. And I'm very good at catching them. I issue more tickets than any of my colleagues.

Speaker 2: I quite enjoy going on tour, appearing in little provincial towns. We sell more tickets in them sometimes, because people don't have so many chances to see live shows. And I get a chance to explore parts of the country I don't know.

Speaker 3: Course I know all the short cuts and that. I get paid by results, so if it means going down one way streets the wrong way sometimes, well … But I don't get caught, and the customers give good tips if deliveries get through faster than they expected.

Speaker 4: These days, it's all electronics, checking computer files, listening to phone calls, as well as reading people's mail, that sort of thing. I have several different passports I use, depending what part of the world I'm operating in. It sounds exciting, I know, but a lot of the work comes down to patience, so it can be pretty boring really.

Speaker 5: The best part is meeting people from different countries – we get all sorts – Japanese, Americans, all parts of Europe. They all ask the same sorts of questions really. Usually I can answer, I'm good on historical background. Sometimes they catch me out, though, on some obscure date!

KEY **Listening practice 4:** Identifying the situation

1

A	B	C	D	E	F
stretch	painful	creamy	plank	seam	frame
repeat	wound	sauce	right-angle	needle	shading
bend	burn	stir	nail	pattern	distance
stand	bandage	heat	saw	stitch	foreground

(*needle* and *stitch* are not really first aid, but rather hospital, *burn* might be cookery, although it shouldn't be!)

2 1 B 2 D 3 F 4 C 5 A

Tapescript

Speaker 1:   ... don't whatever you do use butter, or anything greasy. The vital thing is to cool the area of the burn as rapidly as possible – get it under the cold tap if you can, or pour cold water over it, and don't cover it, because the cloth will have to be unstuck later, and that is likely to be painful, and could lead to ...

Speaker 2:   ... and when you've fixed it securely to the bench, then take the saw and make a small cut underneath, right, making sure it's at right angles to the edge you're cutting, then come back to the top and start sawing through, using your other hand to support the free end of the board. That way, you won't get it splitting under its own weight, which is ...

Speaker 3:   ... you've got everything you need, take your board and find a place to sit where you can see from one room into another. I want you to think today how we can use parts of a building, or perhaps a nearby piece of furniture, to frame something more distant. And I want you to think very carefully about the relative size of things in the foreground and in the background, because ...

Speaker 4:   ... and keep the heat quite high, but don't stop stirring or it'll catch on the bottom and start to burn, you just want it to be brown, not black, and then, when it's changed colour, you can add the liquid and keep on stirring quite energetically until you've got a good, even, creamy sauce. Then, you can put it aside until you've ...

Speaker 5:   ... and now if you set your feet at an angle, about ten to two, like this, yes – not too far apart, and look across to the far wall, lower yourself by bending the knees gently – keep the back as straight as you can, and hold that for a few moments, then slowly up again. And repeat. Go down and hold it a bit longer, good. Can you feel that stretch?

Exam listening

1 Encourage the students to speculate about where the people were and what they might have seen.

2 After they have listened to the tape and checked their answers, ask the students to identify which parts of each speech gave the answers.

KEY	Exam listening			
1 B	2 D	3 F	4 A	5 C

Tapescript

Speaker 1:   It all happened so fast, I hardly had time to realise what was going on. One minute I was looking at some pullovers, and wondering which one to choose …

I'm going on holiday next week, and … anyway, the next minute there were bells ringing and people shouting … but I don't think they caught him. He ran out the back way and into the street, and of course it was crowded, being Saturday …

Speaker 2:   I was on duty up the street from the store when I got a call from the station on my radio. I ran round to the back of the store, but unfortunately I was unable to identify the suspect, as the street was extremely crowded. I was therefore unable to follow him, so I entered the store in order to obtain further details about the crime.

Speaker 3:   Well, there I was, minding my own business, doing a bit of window shopping, when all of a sudden this fellow came racing out of the back of the store. Nearly knocked me over, he did. Course, I didn't get much of a look at him, he was off up the street that fast. I think he had fair hair, or sort of brown, and he was wearing a suit. I think so, anyway.

Speaker 4:   I'd just come back from my tea break, actually. I was helping a gentleman who wanted a tweed jacket – he couldn't find the size he wanted, and then I saw this other man pushing through the crowd near the back doors, and I thought, how rude, then the alarm bells went off and someone shouted. But he was practically in the street by then.

Speaker 5:   I was just thinking I'd had an easy day, in spite of the crowds, it's only my third week. They never had anyone to keep an eye out for shoplifters and such before that, would you credit? Anyway, one of the assistants in perfume called me on my radio to say some guy was behaving suspiciously. I made my way down to the front doors, thinking I'd catch him as he went out of the building. Trouble was, he was heading out the back, but she hadn't told me that …

Unit 8 *Suit yourself*

Timing guide

60–75 mins (Vocabulary: 10–15;   Pronunciation 1: 15–20;
Language practice: 10–15;   Pronunciation 2: 5;
Speaking test practice 1: 10;   Speaking test practice 2: 10)

Revision

If you have time, you could briefly revise some of the vocabulary for
clothing, parts of the body or gestures from Unit 7, as this comes up in
the Odd one out and Speaking test practice activities.

Vocabulary: Odd one out

This exercise revises and extends vocabulary covered in Unit 7. If
students aren't familiar with the type of task, you could do the first one
together as an example

Don't give too much help with vocabulary before or during the exercise
but let students ask for help among themselves, if necessary. Use the
checking phase for thorough clarification of any items students don't
know. Make sure they give reasons for answers and accept alternative
answers which are justified.

KEY   Vocabulary: Odd one out

1 skirt (all the others can be worn by men and women)
2 glove (all the others are worn on the feet)
3 button (all the others are pieces of jewellery)
4 scarf (the only one which is worn separately, and isn't part of a
   coat or jacket)
5 knitted (all the others refer to patterns or designs)
6 neck (all the others are joints)
7 kick (all the others are things you do with hands or arms)
8 wink (all the others are sounds or movements associated with the
   mouth)
9 whisper (all the others refer to eating or drinking)
10 comb (all the others are places to put money)

Pronunciation 1

1 Give students clear models of the three sounds and encourage them to listen carefully and to watch the shape of your mouth as you make the sounds. Make sure they can produce the sounds correctly themselves. Let them repeat the words after the tape for further practice.

2 Students may need help if they find it difficult to hear slight differences on the tape. Again, it's useful for students to repeat the words after the tape.

KEY Pronunciation 1

1 *Group 1* coat whole comb shoulder brooch sole
Group 2 collar wallet sock cough pocket spotted
Group 3 shoe suit chew boot through blue

2 wrist knit climber wrap calm
whole whale salmon comb sign
knee half vehicle honest

Tapescript

1 *Group 1* coat whole comb shoulder brooch sole
Group 2 collar wallet sock cough pocket spotted
Group 3 shoe suit chew boot through blue

2 wrist knit climber wrap calm
whole whale salmon shelf timber
golf half humour comb sign
knee behave vehicle honest ignore

Language practice

This exercise practises the kind of language used to work out what to do and how to do it. As such it's very useful for some of the communication tasks in the First Certificate Speaking test, and also in this book.

KEY Language practice

1 1 d 2 f 3 g 4 i 5 j 6 a 7 b 8 c 9 h 10 e

2 1 e 2 i 3 g 4 j 5 h 6 c 7 f 8 b 9 d 10 a

Tapescript

How shall we begin?
I think we should decide together.
Do you want to start?
Let's discuss each one in turn.
Which is the most important?
Shall we decide about this one first?
Which do you think is the best?
How about starting with this one?
What's your opinion?
I don't know what to do!

Pronunciation 2

The question tag 'shall we?' normally has a rising intonation pattern. Otherwise when question tags are not real questions, they have a falling intonation pattern.

If students find it difficult to hear or imitate the patterns in exercise 1, give them shorter sentences to practise with first. For example,

Falling: This is easy, isn't it? It starts at eight, doesn't it?

Rising: You're not leaving, are you? He didn't hear me, did he?

Tapescript

1

Let's read through the list first, shall we?
We'd better not take too long, had we?
We need to look at the pictures first, don't we?
We've got to put them in order, haven't we?
We can't use all of them, can we?
We could choose a different one, couldn't we?
We'd better check the map, hadn't we?
We'll need to make a decision, won't we?
We don't have to agree about everything, do we?
We haven't missed anything, have we?

2

We can't use all of them, can we?
We don't have to agree about everything, do we?
We haven't missed anything, have we?

Speaking test practice 1: Who gets what?

Remind students of Exam Tip 13, then give them a chance to work out a procedure, hopefully using some of the language they met in the Language practice section of this unit.

Monitor pairs as they work and encourage them to give reasons for the choices they make.

Speaking test practice 2: What's best?

If time allows, at the end of the pair practice, spend a few minutes with the class as a whole, discussing different ways of helping spoken English. Remind them of the discussion arising from exercise 1 on page 5 of their books.

Unit 9 Ideal home

Timing guide

70–75 mins (Pre-listening: 15–20; Listening practice 1: 15; Listening practice 2: 10; Language practice: 10; Exam listening: 20)

Revision

If you have time, you could start by revising vocabulary from the Odd one out exercise (Unit 8) or expressions from the Language practice section (Unit 8).

Pre-listening

1 Give students a few minutes to describe and talk about the cartoon.

Vocabulary which might emerge during feedback includes *tramp, empty/abandoned house, squat/squatter, peeling wallpaper, bare bulb, bare floorboards, spider's web.*

2 Again, give students a few minutes to work through the pictures. If time is short, you could speed up the second task by asking them to discuss which three improvements they would make, if that was all they could do. You could also move those who finish quickly on to question 3 straight away.

3 Ask students to report back on what their partner has told them.

The main appeal is obviously the considerable amount of money that can be saved, but there is also a sense of satisfaction in achieving impressive results from one's own practical skills.

DIY is by no means so popular in all countries and you can develop a class discussion on the reasons for these different attitudes if time allows.

KEY Pre-listening

2 A wallpapering / putting up (or hanging) wallpaper
B painting the walls
C laying a carpet
D making curtains

E changing the light bulb
F making a table
G putting on / fitting a shade
H putting up a shelf

Listening practice 1

1 Allow students to check vocabulary among themselves first, and supply any items which they don't know.

2 One playing should be enough for students to perform this task.

3 This task introduces true/false questions and encourages students to read statements through very carefully. The checking stage provides an opportunity to draw students' attention to some of the common ways of designing statements in this type of question.

Since students have heard the tape once already, they should be able to make some decisions about answers. If they can only answer one or two, this does not matter because the point is that they should know exactly what they are listening for when the tape is played again.

KEY   Listening practice 1

1 A special decorating knives (for scraping and filling)
B paint brushes   **C** white spirit   **D** filler paste   **E** bucket
F tape measure   **G** sandpaper   **H** sponge   **I** undercoat
J gloss paint   **K** paint kettle (a bowl with a handle)   **L** scissors
M cloth

2 All the boxes should be ticked except **E F L**.

3 1 False (Some of them ... but others you may need to buy.)
   Note: This is a typical true/false statement in that it overstates or exaggerates the situation. Words to look out for in such statements are *all/every/always*. It's more likely that *some* or *sometimes* is actually the case.

   2 True (Some people ... life a lot easier if you have the right tools.)
   Note: Here the true statement gives the same information in different words. Often such a statement is shorter and simpler than what is heard on the tape.

   3 True (... but luckily it's not too dear.)
   Note: Another typical kind of statement where an alternative word (or phrase) is used.

   4 False (You could use any suitable bowl really.)

   5 True (cleaning brushes ... and thinning paint)

   6 False (There are lots of kinds on the market.)

   7 True (... in different widths)

   8 False (Make sure you buy enough ... run out half way through.)

Tapescript

L: Lynn (Instructress); S1: Student 1; S2: Student 2

L: Right, Mr Anderson will be showing you how to use gloss paint in a minute and giving you a demonstration, hopefully, but first I'll show you the equipment you're going to need. Can you all gather round? Good…Evening Len.

S1: Oh, sorry I'm late.

L: Not to worry, We've only just started. Well, on the table here you can see the essentials. Now some of them you've probably got at home already but others you may need to buy. OK, first there's an ordinary sponge – a clean one, mind – and a piece of cloth of some kind. I'm sure you've all got those somewhere. Next we have a scraping knife with quite a wide blade. It's for removing old paint and wallpaper. The one with the narrow blade is a filling knife. Some people use ordinary knives but you'll make life a lot easier if you have the right tools. Next some sheets of sandpaper for smoothing surfaces down. You'll need a selection of different grades, coarse and fine, but luckily it's not too dear to buy. Uh, any questions?

S2: Yes, what's this bowl here?

L: I was coming to that. It's what's called a paint *kettle* and it's basically a bowl with a handle. You could use any suitable bowl really. It's for holding the paint while you work. Now here we have a bottle of ordinary white spirit…

S1: For cleaning brushes?

L: Right, and thinning the paint if necessary. And a tub of filler for filling cracks and holes. There are lots of kinds on the market. Um, what's left?

S2: Brushes?

L: Yes, you'll need some good quality paint brushes in different widths and, of course, the paint of your choice – undercoat and gloss. Make sure you buy enough to finish the job. You don't want to run out half way through, and you can always use leftovers for touching up later. Ah, here's Mr Anderson now. Over to you Cecil.

Listening practice 2

1 Check with students that they understand what is meant by a self-assembly kit.

2 When checking answers with the class, draw attention to the rubric (i.e. according to what Bill actually says) and to the way the true/false statements are worded.

KEY Listening practice 2

1 False (You should check the size of the *place where you're going to put the bookcase.*)

2 True (some stores will deliver without charge)

3 False (… if you have to buy … specialist tools, … spending more on them than on the bookcase. You should be able to manage with just a screwdriver and a hammer … and they're useful things to have anyway.) He contrasts 'specialist tools' with *'just* a screwdriver and a hammer'.

4 True (He says you must protect the floor.)

5 False (He tells you to check that it's complete *by reading* the instructions.)

6 True (Do follow the instructions. … don't leave bits out.)

7 False (He says if it doesn't fit, it's you who's wrong, not the kit. You've probably got the wrong bit, or it's upside down or something.)

Tapescript

A: And now here on *College Sound*, we're going to look into the practical side of fixing up your room. One of the things that everyone finds is that they soon run out of space for books. Now you can keep them in piles on the floor, or you can hunt around the junk shops for a second-hand bookcase. But one quick and quite cheap solution is to make your own with a self-assembly kit. Bill's here to give us a few hints. Bill, we've all heard disaster stories about this sort of stuff, what do we need to do to avoid ending up with a sore thumb and three bits of wood on the floor?

B: OK. The first thing is to plan. Check the size of the space you have before you go shopping. You don't want to get involved in trying to alter the size of the thing, shorten the shelves or something, that's a job to be left for the Do-it-yourself expert. Then try to visit more than one shop before you buy. You can often find some really cheap stuff, but you need to be sure it's right for you. And some stores will deliver without charge, which is important if you haven't got a car, or a mate who's got one. And before you buy, look carefully at the samples on display. Try to see how they're put together. Fancy ones may look good, but if you have to buy a load of specialist tools, you can easily end up spending more on them than on the bookcase. You should be able to manage with just a screwdriver and possibly a hammer. These can be very cheap, if you can't borrow them, and they're useful things to have anyway.

The next thing is to work methodically. Allow plenty of time – don't believe the blurb on the box which says 'ready in ten minutes' – that's not how it'll be. Start by protecting the floor, specially if you've got a landlady, newspapers will do for this, so it doesn't get scratched or cut. Then unpack very, very carefully.

Lay everything out tidily and look at the instructions. Now – don't do anything. Get yourself a cup of coffee and go through all the instructions, identifying every piece of wood, every screw, every little bit of plastic or sachet of glue. If there's anything missing, go straight back to the shop now. It's no good when the thing's half made!

Once you're sure you've got all the bits, you're ready to start. And here you need to beware, you've really got to follow the instructions. If they tell you to put the back on last, or first, there'll be a reason for it. If something doesn't seem to fit, don't force it. Check again. You've probably got the wrong bit, or it's upside down or something. And don't leave bits out. It may look all right with only two screws done up, but if it's supposed to have four, it probably needs them. You don't want it all to come crashing down in the middle of the night.

A: Well, thanks Bill. You've obviously learnt from experience. Now before our next piece of advice, here's some music …

Language practice: Vocabulary: Adjectives into verbs

This exercise can be skipped or set for homework if you're short of time.

KEY   Vocabulary: Adjectives into verbs

1	tighten	6	loosen
2	widen	7	roughened
3	straighten	8	blackened
4	lengthen (NB opposite = shorten)	9	whiten
5	darken	10	redden

Exam listening: Legal advice

It's important to insist that students read through the instructions and statements very carefully.

The instructions set the scene and so make the listening process easier. Point out that time can be lost and answers to questions missed if you are wondering what on earth is going on!

When students have had time to read through the question, ask comprehension questions on the task. For example:

– What two people are you going to hear speaking?
– Do they know each other?
– Why has Sandra called the advice line?
– What kind of problem has she got? (judging from the T/F statements)

Give students an opportunity to ask questions about any problem vocabulary in the statements, if necessary. Obviously this is not possible in a real exam, but it will encourage them to read carefully and to start from a position of confidence. If students do ask questions, help them to work out the meanings for themselves, if possible.

KEY   **Exam listening:** Legal advice

1 False (She has had <u>one</u> room redecorated.)
2 False (This is not mentioned.)
3 False (The reason given is that he didn't mix it well enough. We don't know that he bought the paint and Sandra doesn't say that it was the wrong colour, but rather that there were two different shades of yellow.)
4 True (The line where the walls meet the ceiling isn't straight.)
5 True (he didn't have enough sheets to put down on the floor.)
6 True (Alternative word: *fussy*)
7 True (This summarises his advice: ... that you require him to repaint the ceilings... a wavy line)
8 False (She should ask for an invoice.)
9 True (agree a reduction)
10 False (She should ask someone to give her an estimate for doing the work.)

Tapescript

S: Sandra; M: Mr Montgomery

M: Hello, this is Mr Montgomery speaking. I specialise in litigation. I understand you have a problem with a builder. Could you tell me about it?
S: Yes, I, er, I hope you can help me. I...I've had my living room decorated, and the painter has made rather a mess of it really. And I don't quite know what I should do now. I don't know whether to pay him or not.
M: Did he give you a quote?
S: Yes, yes he did. He gave me a quote before he started the work.
M: How much was it for?
S: He said it would be about £500.
M: Well did he say exactly £500, or round about £500, or £500 plus VAT?
S: Er...it was, I think it was £505 plus VAT.
M: What did you instruct him to do?
S: To paint the living room walls, and the ceiling, um and to paint the sort of paintwork as well, you know the skirting boards and things like that.
M: And what's the problem?

S: Well, he's made an awful mess of it really. I mean, he had to paint the walls yellow, but he's managed to paint them two different shades of yellow, really, so when you walk in, it looks as if one wall's a different colour from the other one. He didn't, he didn't mix it well enough so they don't match very well. That's one thing. Um, and another thing is that the line where the walls meet the ceiling isn't straight. So he sometimes, the paint goes over on to the ceiling and sometimes it doesn't. It looks terrible. Um...

M: So you're unhappy with it?

S: I'm unhappy with it, yes, and he also kept spilling paint all over the carpet because he didn't have enough sheets to put down on the floor. So it's made rather a mess of the carpet and I don't know if I can get that cleaned or not.

M: Have you spoken to him about this?

S: Yes.

M: And what's he said?

S: He doesn't seem to think there's anything wrong with it. He seems to think I'm being very fussy.

M: Right. Well, your position is this: you are in the strongest position because he wants your money, and you haven't paid him anything, yet. My advice to you is not to pay him anything, to tell him that you've taken advice and that you require the walls to be done again in the shade that you want it to be done, that you require him to clean the carpets and that you require him to repaint the ceiling and the wall where they meet such that the line becomes a straight line and not a wavy line. Uh, he may or may not decide to do that. If he says 'No, I've done a good job', then uh, if he's in your house and you're worried about him being there, I suggest you ask for his invoice. And then, when his invoice comes, you can write to him and you can tell him that you're not happy with it, and you're not going to pay him.

S: So you don't think I should pay him anything, then?

M: I don't think you should pay him anything because he hasn't done what you asked him to do, and he therefore appears to be in breach of contract. But not only that, he appears to have damaged your carpet and you may have to pay somebody to have that carpet cleaned. Of course another possibility is that you could just negotiate a reduction. Get him off your hands and with the difference, employ somebody else to put it right and somebody else to clean the carpet. But you'd obviously have to have somebody to come in to give you an estimate prior to your negotiations with that builder to agree a reduction.

S: Right. OK thank you very much.

Unit 10 Upstairs, downstairs

Timing guide

70–75 mins (Vocabulary: 25; Pronunciation: 15;
Language practice: 15; Speaking test practice 1 and 2: 15–20)

Revision

If time, revise some of the DIY vocabulary or -en verbs from Unit 9.

Vocabulary

You could introduce the topic, before students open their books, by writing the following words on the board (stopping after each group of three) and asking if students can guess what they all refer to:

charming	traditional	views
magnificent	modern	gardens
luxury	17th century	grounds

1 Start checking from the words the students didn't know. Let them ask about any other related vocabulary they want to know as well.

KEY Vocabulary

1 A chimney **B** aerial **C** loft/attic **D** drainpipe
E top/second floor **F** stairs/staircase **G** first floor
H ground floor **I** garage **J** basement **K** steps **L** hedge
M drive(way) **N** path **O** fence

---

2 When checking, make sure students can distinguish between the different types of house: *cottage*, *bungalow*, *detached house*, *terrace(d house)*, *semi-detached*, etc.

After a few minutes, ask students to report back on what their partners have told them.

KEY Vocabulary

2 1 H   2 C   3 G   4 B   5 D   6 E   7 F   8 A

58

Talking about your neighbourhood

Start this section by checking with students that they know how to form appropriate questions for each part of the form. You may also like to suggest a few possibilities for the 'other' categories, if appropriate.

Pronunciation 1

1 Introduce this 'minimal pairs' activity by pronouncing a few of the words yourself and asking students to say which list they are from. It's important that they should be able to hear a difference before they try to produce distinct sounds themselves.

If students have little or no difficulty with the sounds, go through the exercises quickly. If any students have real problems with producing two distinct sounds, help them as far as possible but don't labour the point.

2 Make sure students can write the phonetic symbols. The exercise tests sound/spelling relationships as much as it practises pronunciation.

Note: These words are not included on the tape as the key sounds would be difficult to distinguish in a recording.

KEY Pronunciation 1

1 bedrooms /z/   houses /ɪz/   stairs /z/   lifts /s/   bungalows /z/
flats /s/   parks /s/   steps /s/   cottages /ɪz/   shops /s/   floors /z/
gardens /z/   lounges /ɪz/   kitchens /z/   fences /ɪz/

2 special /ʃ/   machine /ʃ/   vision /ʒ/   station /ʃ/   occasion /ʒ/
moustache /ʃ/   leisure /ʒ/   garage /ʒ/   chalet /ʃ/   beige /ʒ/

Language practice

1 Make sure that students are clear about the usage of these words, several of which may be 'false friends'.

Give clear models to help them identify the word stress.

Encourage students to note any occupations which they might want to mention in their Speaking test, when talking about themselves or their families.

KEY Language practice

1 engineer   accountant   lawyer   mechanic   bank cashier

home help   professor   lecturer   chemist   security guard

social worker   estate agent

---

2 Draw students' attention to the tenses used in the answers. If necessary, discuss briefly the reasons for using the present perfect simple/continuous.

Tapescript

Can you tell me about your grandmother?
She's worked at the local primary school for thirty years, but now she's retiring.
And what about your older sister?
She's a research chemist for a big international company.
How long has she been there?
She's been working there since she finished her degree.
And your other sister?
She's been working as a cashier at the supermarket since she left school last summer.

Pronunciation 2: Longer sentences

1 Play the tape and encourage students to repeat the target language with correct stress and intonation.

2 Monitor pairs as they work, checking their sentence stress and noting examples. If possible, spend a few minutes practising some of these with the whole class either now or in a subsequent lesson.

Tapescript

She's worked at the local primary school for thirty years, but now she's retiring.
She's a research scientist for a big international company.
She's been working there since she finished her degree.
She's been working as a cashier at the supermarket since she left school last summer.

Speaking test practice 1

Make sure that students understand what they have to do before they start and encourage them to answer each other's questions as fully as possible.

Speaking test practice 2

Encourage imaginative and light-hearted suggestions. If time allows, when students have finished, have a brief class discussion on noise pollution, encouraging students to contribute their own experiences and opinions.

Unit 11 Talking shop

Timing guide
60–70 mins (Pre-listening: 20–25;   Listening practice: 20–25;
Exam listening: 20)

Revision

If you have time, revise some vocabulary related to houses (e.g.
loft/attic, *basement*, *drive* etc.) or ways of complaining from Unit 10.

Pre-listening

1 It's best to ask students to cover the answers at the bottom of the
page initially unless their level is fairly low.

When checking answers, distinguish between *stationery* and
stationer's, and *jewellery* and *jeweller's*. Ask students to give examples
of *stationery* (e.g. notepaper, envelopes, glue) and *jewellery* (e.g.
brooch, bracelet, necklace). Point out, however, that in the case of
baker/baker's and *grocery/grocer's* both words refer to the shop.

Check and practise the pronunciation of *stationery* and *jewellery*. You
could also give extra practice of the /s/ and /z/ '-s' endings if you feel
your students need it.

2 Allow a few minutes for students to discuss these points (explain
bargain if necessary). Ask a few students to report back on their
preferences, but keep this stage fairly brief.

3 You could use the checking phase of this activity to remind students
about other road features e.g. *fast/slow lane, northbound/southbound
carriageway, dead end* etc.

KEY   Pre-listening

1 A tobacconist's   **B** pet shop   **C** hardware shop   **D** stationer's
E fishmonger's   **F** jeweller's   **G** newsagent's   **H** bakery (or
baker's)   **I** grocer's   **J** greengrocer's

3 A roundabout   **B** level crossing   **C** bend (NB not curve)
D (T) junction   **E** pedestrian or (zebra) crossing   **F** fork
G crossroads   **H** flyover

Listening practice 1

Ask students to look through the diagrams first and think about the directions which are shown first. Pause the tape briefly between instructions to give them time to locate answers, and play a second time if necessary. When checking answers, get students to give the correct instruction in each case.

KEY   Listening practice 1

1 1 **D**   2 **G**   3 **F**   4 **B**   5 **I**   6 **C**   7 **H**   8 **A**   9 **E**

2 J Take the third turning on the right.
  K Turn left at the T-junction.
  L Go round the roundabout and take the third exit.

Tapescript

1 It's the first turning on the left.
2 Go straight on till you reach the T-junction.
3 Go round the roundabout and take the second exit.
4 Turn right at the traffic lights and you'll see it on the left.
5 When you come to a fork in the road, branch left.
6 Go straight across the crossroads.
7 Turn sharp left.
8 Go past the bridge.
9 Turn right at the junction.

Listening practice 2

If students are new to multiple choice questions, go through the preparation stage with the whole class before playing the tape. All the passages are heard twice on the tape as in the exam.

After the second listening it may be useful to discuss vocabulary clues with the whole class too.

KEY   Listening practice 2

1 B   2 B   3 C   4 B   5 A

Tapescript

Man: I need a copy of this document right away.
Receptionist: Yes, sir. Um, if you go down the road and turn left...
Man: By the newsagent's?
Receptionist: That's it. The local library will do it for ten pence a sheet. Our machine is playing up at the moment and we've called the engineer. Otherwise I'd be happy to make a copy here for you, sir, if it was just the one page.

Woman: Well, I was in there last week, but I'm not in any hurry to go again. It's not their fault, poor things. They try to find something to suit you, but it's no use saying everything's dead cheap if there's nothing worth looking at.

Man: The post office? Yes, it's not far. When you get to the next crossroads turn right into the High Street. Carry on along the High Street and then take the second left into Long Lane. You can't miss the turning. There's a pub called the Old Crown on the corner. The post office is on the left, a bit further down that road.

Customer: Are these the only lemon biscuits you've got?
Shopkeeper: They are.
Customer: They're a bit too sweet for my taste. We got some in London which were better.
Shopkeeper: Well, if you tell me the brand, we could try and order them for you.
Customer: That'd be great. If I can just remember. Tell you what, I'll get my sister to send me a packet and you can see what they're like for yourself.
Shopkeeper: Well, if it's no trouble. We're always interested in trying new ranges.

Cashier: I'll have to leave the check-out, I'm afraid. Nobody's ever spoken to me like that in my life. I don't care who he is, he has no right to say such a thing. And in front of customers too. I really don't think I can carry on to the end of my shift.
Supervisor: Okay. I'll get someone to take over from you. And then we'd better talk to the manager.

Exam listening

Draw students' attention to Exam Tip 18 and let them hear the tape twice before going through the answers.

KEY   Exam listening

1 B   2 C   3 A   4 A   5 C   6 B   7 C

Tapescript

S: Sue; C: Charles

S: Well Charles, I must say that your shop is pretty remarkable. Um, it's basically a sweetshop, but you also do stationery and greetings cards and tobacco and fireworks...

C: And newspapers.

S: And newspapers. I mean is there anything you don't sell?

C: Yes, shoelaces. (*laughter*) I haven't got round to shoelaces yet.

S: But you've had some requests for that?

C: One or two but I tend, I tend to send them into the hardware shop next door.

S: Ah. And apart from all that, you've got photocopiers...

C: That's right.

S: Two.

C: Yes.

S: And a fax machine.

C: Indeed.

S: Yes. How did... I mean. Why the photocopiers?

C: Everything that's happened in my shop has almost happened by accident. But when I got into Clifton, I needed a photocopy one day and no one could tell me where to go. So it struck me that if I didn't know where to go, other people were in the same situation, so that's why I started it. And I had one, and it was an old machine, and then I got two, and now they're better and they enlarge and they reduce in size, and then I added on a facsimile machine because it seemed like a natural progression at the time. And all sorts of people use it.

S: Yes, who, what sort of people do use it?

C: Um, a lot of professional people – surveyors, engineers – particularly people who need to send plans. Because in the past you could send messages via telex, but a telex can't express a plan, whereas facsimile has that dimension, the added dimension.

S: Right. And do people send these fax messages abroad, or is it just to this country?

C: Well, it's surprising because when I started, I thought I'd be sending things to London and maybe Birmingham but, in fact, a high percentage of it is sent abroad, because it's immediate, it's very speedy. You can send a message one day and, if it's into a different time zone, you might gain and then you have a message back very quickly

S: And how much would it cost, for example, if I wanted to send a fax to the United States?

C: Well, a fax to the United States would cost you five pounds for a page. And when you think that in England by the Royal Mail, it would cost you twelve pounds to send a page by special delivery, it's actually good value.

S: OK. What about your hours? How long do you have to spend actually in the shop?

C: Well, the shop is open from, essentially from eight in the morning until six at night, six days a week, and then a sort of fairly flexible morning on a Sunday. Um, and of those hours, I'm in it quite a lot.

S: And how long have you actually had the shop?

C: Well, I took over the shop in 1982, 22nd December, it sort of, no, sorry, 22nd November – it sticks in my brain.

S: And do you enjoy it?

C: Yes, overall I enjoy it. Running a business by yourself is jolly hard work and you never quite like every aspect all the time. 95% of the customers I love. Uh, 2% I really, you know, I'm not too bothered about. And 3% I positively hate.

S: What, what's the problem with those? Are they people who stay around and talk to you when you're busy or complain or what?

C: Um, it's hard to categorise really. I find people who are just totally rude, um, unnecessary, and I don't really need their custom. And I suppose they form the volume of the people that I don't like. But it's a very, very, very small percentage.

S: But is there a danger that shops like yours will disappear, more and more?

C: I think there's a very, very great danger that the majority of them will disappear.

S: Why's that?

C: Simply because costs of running a shop have just become very, very high. To give you some example, in the time that I've been there, my rent has quadrupled, my rates have doubled, other costs have gone up proportionately. And at the end of the day it is a little bit hard to try and keep up with those costs. You can, certainly you can extend the volume of your sales but they don't necessarily always catch up with the costs. But, having said that, I mean there will always be successful small shops, so I hope that I'm in that category.

S: Yes, and is there anything...do you think anything can be done to stop this trend?

C: Yes, change the government. (*laughter*)

S: That's what it comes down to.

C: I'm afraid that's what it comes down to. Now a small shopkeeper should...

Unit 12 You only live once

Timing guide

70–80 mins (Discussion / Pronunciation: 20;   Language practice: 30;
Speaking test practice 1: 10–15; Speaking test practice 2: 10–15)

Revision

If you have time, you could begin by revising some words connected
with shops or road features from Unit 11. It's best not to revise
directions at this stage since they are recycled later in the unit.

Discussion

1 Monitor students through activities 1, 2 and 3 to ensure that they
understand what they have to do. You may like to check whether
everyone finds the same pattern. Theoretically, it should be:

	more / less common	active / inactive
a) playing computer games	✔	I
b) running errands for their parents	✔	A
c) watching sport on television	✔	I
d) playing football with friends	✔	A
e) using the internet	✔	I
f) riding a bicycle	✔	A
g) watching videos	✔	I
h) exploring the countryside	✔	A

Discuss any divergence of opinion.
Have a brief class discussion about 3. The causes of weight problems in
children can be drawn from 1 and 2, and are connected with modern,
mainly urban, lifestyles. The main reason it matters is that being
overweight in childhood increases the risk of poor health in later life,
especially heart disease. (The reason for confining the discussion to
childhood is to avoid making any members of the class feel victimised,
but be wary of this.)

2 You may wish to pre-teach some vocabulary for your students' leisure activities (names of sports, etc.) and revise relevant structures, such as I play tennis / I play the guitar, I go swimming / I do aerobics.

The quiz should be regarded lightheartedly. If appropriate, there could be a 'competition' between halves of the class, or boys and girls, to see which has the healthier lifestyle, based on the answers given during the pairwork.

Pronunciation: Stress in words

Make sure students practise the correct stress patterns of any words which caused problems after checking their answers.

KEY Pronunciation: Stress in words

□	□	□	□	□
concerned	activity	exploring	lifestyle	internet
□	□	□	□	□
computer	overweight	seriously	disease	increasingly

Tapescript

concerned	activity	exploring	lifestyle	internet
computer	overweight	seriously	disease	increasingly

Language practice 1: Talking about future plans

1 Make sure students know what they have to do. Check the answers with the class before they go on to 2 and 3.

KEY Language practice 1: Talking about future plans

	Yes	Perhaps	No
1 I'm hoping to …		✗	
2 I'm going to …	✗		
3 I shall probably …	✗		
4 There's a possibility that I may …		✗	
5 I'd like to …		✗	
6 It's unlikely I'll ever …			✗
7 I certainly wouldn't want to …			✗

While they are doing 4, go round offering help with any language they need to talk about their own plans.

Tapescript

1 I'm hoping to go to college.
2 I'm going to college.
3 I shall probably go to college.
4 There's a possibility I may go to college.
5 I'd like to go to college.
6 It's unlikely I'll ever go to college.
7 I certainly wouldn't want to go to college.

Language practice 2: Talking about what other people should do

1 Remind students of Unit 10, Speaking test practice 2. Here are ways we can talk about what we think other people should do.

Tapescript

1 I think he should take more exercise.
2 In my opinion he ought to relax more.
3 What he needs to do is go on a diet.
4 What he needs to do is eat less chocolate.
5 What he needs to do is give up smoking.

2 Encourage imaginative and amusing as well as realistic suggestions, as long as students use the target language.

Speaking test practice 1

Make sure that students know what they have to do. Remind them of the language practised in Language practice 1 of this unit and also in Unit 10 Language practice 1.

Speaking test practice 2

This follows on from Language practice 2. You may like to spend a few minutes discussing Alice's appearance with the class, before asking them to discuss in pairs what she should do.

Unit 13 Travelling light

Timing guide

75–85 mins (Pre-listening: 15;   Listening practice 1: 15;
Listening practice 2: 15–20;   Vocabulary: 5–10;
Language practice: 10; Exam listening: 15)

Revision

If you have time, you could revise ways of giving directions or asking a favour from Unit 12.

Pre-listening

1 Give students a few moments to look at and discuss the drawings and help with any words they don't know e.g.

E bathrobe   **K** portable computer   **S** money belt
U notepad / writing paper and envelopes.

2 a) An alternative approach here is to ask students to choose a journey for their partner (this tends to ensure that a greater variety of journeys is chosen). They could swap books for a moment and underline the chosen details in their partner's book. Check that everyone is clear about the details of their journey by asking one or two people to say where they're going and why.

b) Keep this phase fairly brief by giving a time limit of about 2 mins.

c) Give students a few minutes to ask questions and then tell them to explain their other choices to their partners. Monitor to encourage them to ask questions and challenge reasons, e.g.

Do you really think you need to take a towel to your friend's house? Why will you need an umbrella in California? Don't you think you'll need a guidebook?

Ask one or two people to report back on some of their partner's choices and reasons. This calls for a change of discourse and provides a general incentive to listen carefully in pair discussions! You could structure this feedback by looking at each of the main purposes for the journey.

KEY   Pre-listening

1 A iron
B bank/credit card
C personal stereo
D umbrella
E bathrobe
F camera
G towel
H torch
I dectective novel
J sunglasses
K portable computer
L map

M first aid kit
N calculator
O teddy bear / toy
P phrase book
Q sun oil / sun tan lotion
R travel washing line
S money belt
T guidebook
U notepad / writing paper
  and envelopes
V present
W penknife

Listening practice 1

1 Get students to name each of the types of luggage and ask for brief comments on advantages and disadvantages.

2 The intention here is to encourage predictive listening. If students think about the topic area and possible answers in advance, they will be better tuned to topic vocabulary and ideas when they listen. This also makes the listening process more interesting and motivating.

Encourage them to make a few suggestions – either in pairs or to the class as a whole – as to how they pack clothes so that they don't get too creased, how they make the most of the available space, etc.

3 Stop the tape for a few seconds between extracts. Allow students to compare answers and play the recording through a second time if necessary.

Ask students to say what extra kind of luggage was mentioned on the tape and to write it next to the question mark at F.

KEY   Listening practice 1

1 A suitcase
B suit carrier
C rucksack / backpack

D holdall
E (cabin) trunk
F ? = sausage bag

3 1 Take as little as possible.
  2 Use a sausage bag instead of a suitcase.
  3 Have a list of everything you need to take and tick things off as you put them in. (Also to make use of every bit of space e.g. by putting socks and underwear into shoes.)
  4 Get somebody else to do it.

Tapescript

1 Well, I'm useless at packing suitcases so for me the secret of successful suitcase packing is to take as little as possible with you.

2 I think the secret to successful suitcase packing is not to have a suitcase. Have a sausage bag and just stuff everything in it, and then when it goes on buses and trains and planes, people can throw it about, things don't get broken, that's the trick.

3 Well the art of really successful suitcase packing is to have a list of everything that you intend to take with you, and then to put it in and tick things off. And of course one always stuffs things like socks and underwear into shoes and things like that so you're making use of every available bit of space. However, it has to be said that it's very easy to pack when you're going away but there always seems to be far too much stuff when you're coming back.

4 I'm hopeless at packing suitcases so my secret is – get somebody else to do it for me.

Listening practice 2

1 Give students a few minutes to exchange experiences and then invite one or two to tell their partner's story to the class.

2 Again the intention is to encourage students to scan the questions for information which helps them predict what the story is going to be about. It's probably best to take the items one at a time or in two pairs. Ask for suggestions in each case and encourage sensible ideas.

3 Students can answer the questions as they listen and you could discuss a few other general points, but very detailed questions would not be appropriate.

KEY   Listening practice 2

1 A 1 two days   2 was leaving   3 ticket   4 temporary
   B 1 B   2 D   3 C
   C 1 False   2 False   3 True   4 True
   D 1 B   2 D

Tapescript

A Well, one of the worst experiences I had was at the very end of a long six-month holiday, a very long way away from home. And I'd booked an airflight home, and two days before the flight was about to leave, I had my passport and my airline ticket stolen and I had very very little money left. And, um, so I went to the um, British Embassy to try and get a new ticket, a new passport, and they said they could only give me a passport if I could prove I was leaving – and I didn't have my ticket. So I went to the airline and they said I could only have a new ticket if I could prove who I was, but I didn't have a passport. So I was in a bit of a tricky situation. But I finally did get a temporary passport from the embassy and I finally flew home.

B I was riding a motorcycle in Bali, in Indonesia, and got hopelessly lost, and it was teeming with rain and I was very depressed and trying to find my way out, and through my pronunciation of the name of a certain town, I got given directions to the wrong side of the island, because I was pronouncing the town I actually wanted to be in wrongly and people were quite genuinely thinking they were giving me the right directions, and I ended up, you know, fifty miles away from where I was meant to be.

C Well my bad experience happened some years ago when I was a student and I was with a group of friends on an InterRail holiday. And we were sitting in a café and one person had the bag with all the passports and money and everything in it, and we left the café and this person forgot the bag. We then went back to the café – the bag wasn't there. So all of us had lost our InterRail tickets, our passports and all our money. So we were desperately upset, as you can imagine. We went to the British Consul and they organised money from our parents, and sorted us out, and we were due to fly home the next morning. Anyway, the next morning, on the way to the airport, we were actually on the bus on the way to the airport, and we passed a police station. And as we passed the police station, Mark, one of the people in the group, said 'There is a man walking up the steps of the police station with the bag.' And we went, 'Don't be daft!' And he said 'There is! There is, it's the bag!' And he was so convincing that he managed to persuade us all to get off the bus and go the police station. And when we went into the police station, he was right, the bag had just been handed in. So we were able to get our passports, our money, our InterRail tickets back, and carry on with our holiday.

D My worst holiday experience, as I recall, was in a particular country – I was hitch-hiking around with a rucksack on my back, and I got dropped off by someone, thinking I was near a town only to find that I was literally in the middle of nowhere, and it was getting dark. So I chose a camping site and pulled my tent out and put it up, only to find that I'd, I was camping in the middle of the most incredible mosquito-breeding ground I've ever seen. And my tent was very quickly absolutely chock-a-block full of thousands of mosquitoes. Of course I had no aerosols, no nothing to get rid of mosquitoes at all. It was quite a warm evening and I had to climb inside my very hot sleeping bag and leave just a quarter of an inch to breathe through, and still ended up being eaten alive – they still managed to get into my sleeping bag!

Vocabulary: Guessing unknown words and phrases

If you are short of time, read from the tapescript to remind students of the context rather than play the tape again.

> **KEY**   **Vocabulary:** Guessing unknown words and phrases
>
> a) a situation that's difficult to deal with
> b) it was raining very heavily
> c) don't be silly/stupid
> d) it was completely full of...

Language practice: Phrasal verbs

Advise students to look at the sentences first, rather than try to match verbs and participles from the lists. Monitor and point out the need to put verbs in the correct tense as necessary.

> **KEY**   **Language practice:** Phrasal verbs
>
> 1 sorted us out   4 dropped off
> 2 handed in   5 pulled my tent out; put it up
> 3 carry on   6 ended up

Exam listening

Let the students work through the Preparation stage in pairs, then discuss their answers to 3 with the whole class. Draw their attention to the rubric, especially the names of the three books. It's also worth pointing out to them that the questions will always be in the same order as the information is presented in the text.

After they have listened twice, check the answers with them and discuss which parts of the recording gave the answers.

> **KEY**   Exam listening
>
> 1 A   2 C   3 B   4 B   5 C   6 A   7 C

Unit 13 **Travelling light**

Tapescript

B: Today we're winding up the programme by looking at three series of guides for tourists. And I've got Angie Knox here to help me. Angie.

A: Hi. Well, first of all there's *Astin's*, which has been well-known to generations of tourists. It's packed with all the sorts of places you could possibly want to know about, from museums to motor way service stations. In comparison, the other two, *Brisk Tours* and *Explore in Comfort* are only skimming the surface …

B: But that does make them a bit more practical to carry about with you if you're not travelling by car, doesn't it?

A: Well, yes. And another thing about *Astin's* is that, although it tells you where the bus and railway stations are, it's clearly geared to the traveller with plenty of money for taxis and so on, as it gives only basic guidelines about whether out of the way attractions can be reached by public transport.

B: Yes, and I would say *Brisk Tours* is also very much a driver's guide.

A: Oh, it makes no claim to be otherwise, I'd say. But *Explore in Comfort* is actually very good on the hows and whens of getting around with or without a car, and it has a good section on how to check information about timetables and so on…

B: Rather than offering facts which may have changed by the time you get there.

A: *Brisk Tours* tries to do a similar thing, but unfortunately, they don't seem to be much good at double-checking phone numbers and quite a lot of the codes are wrong.

B: Really?

A: Yes. But *Brisk Tours* is good on suggesting trouble free routes for the motorist. Although it would be worth waiting for the new editions later in the year if you can, as there have been so many changes to the motorway system since the current one came out.

B: Right. And for me, I'd say it's also the easiest of the three to find what you want in quickly, with a good index and really clear layout.

A: *Astin's* and *Explore* are both alphabetical by city, which can be inconvenient…

B: And *Explore* doesn't always present the local information in the same order for each area, which can be really confusing.

A: I didn't notice that, but I should think it could be really irritating. On the other hand, it has some of the best maps I've seen for a long time, which is more than can be said for the other two.

B: Oh, absolutely. *Brisk Tours* are much too general and *Astin's* are in such tiny print you need a magnifying glass.

A: Considering it's so much more expensive than the others, you'd think they could spend a bit more on print quality.

B: Yeah, so, well, *Brisk Tours* is the cheapest, and it has <u>some</u> good points.

A: Well, a few good points, I suppose, but for general reliability, *Explore* is well worth the extra couple of pounds, I'd say. Wouldn't you agree?

B: Oh yes, I would. So, there you go. Thank you Angie.

A: Thank you.

B: And happy holidays!

74

Unit 14 It's your world

Timing guide
55–70 mins (Exam discussion: 10–15;   Language practice: 20;
Pronunciation 2: 5–10;   Speaking test practice 1: 10–15;
Speaking test practice 2: 10)

Revision
If you have time, revise Unit 2 structures with *whereas/while,* Unit 6
comparing and contrasting and Unit 4 giving reasons for opinions.

Exam discussion
This practice draws together work from earlier units.

1 The contrast is not only in the food, but also in the amount of
packaging which is less environmentally friendly.

2 Comparing lists with other pairs may offer motivation in the form of
friendly competition.

3 You may like to go through Exam Tip 22 with the whole class before
they do this pair practice. Restrict this to a brief practice, just enough
to familiarise students with the pictures. They will return to them in
Language practice 1 part 3.

Language practice 1
Refer students to Exam Tip 22. Make sure students understand that the
sentences in Exercises 1 and 2 do not refer to pictures in the Student's
Book.

Check that they have correctly matched the four parts of the description
with the examples before they move on to 2.

KEY   Language practice 1

1 A 3   B 1   C 4   D 2

2 although they're both houses, one's much more modern
there are a lot of people in both photos
personally, I'd love to travel like this
both groups of people are laughing
these people seem to be looking forward to something, but those
aren't

I imagine they must be feeling cold
both streets are busy, but this one has fewer private cars
this room is clean and tidy, but this one's a mess

Language practice 2: Expressing a different point of view

If necessary, briefly practise expressions of agreement.

1 Check that students know what they have to do and monitor the pairs as they match the sentences.

Pronunciation 1

2 Practise with the whole class, emphasising the polite intonation.

3 It may be a good idea to go through the first half of the list of opinions with the whole class and then let them do the second half on their own, before beginning the pair practice.

If further practice seems advisable and time allows, students could have some fun furnishing outrageous statements for each other to disagree with.

Tapescript

1 Actually, I don't believe that the situation is hopeless.
2 But don't you think some cars are necessary?
3 I'm afraid I don't agree that that's the best solution.
4 On the other hand, maybe they aren't always practical for older people.

Pronunciation 2

Give students clear models of the three sounds and encourage them to listen carefully and to watch the shape of your mouth as you make the sounds. Make sure they can produce the sounds correctly themselves. Let them repeat the sounds after the tape for further practice.

KEY	Pronunciation 2					
Group 1	money	cover	fuss	enough	colour	country
Group 2	foot	put	could	good	pull	look
Group 3	torch	abroad	thought	course	sort	walk

Tapescript

Group 1 money cover fuss enough colour country
Group 2 foot put could good pull look
Group 3 torch abroad thought course sort walk

Speaking test practice 1

Before students begin, check that they understand all the language in the poster.

Make sure they read the rubric carefully and know what they have to do. Reassure them that there are no 'correct' and 'incorrect' opinions, but remind them that they must give reasons for their views.

Speaking test practice 2

You may wish to point out to students that this exercise develops out of Speaking practice 1 in the way that Part 4 of the Speaking test develops out of Part 3.

Remind them again that they should always give reasons for any opinions they offer.

When they have finished, if time allows, have a brief class discussion on some of the issues raised.

Unit 15 Listening review

Timing guide

65–75 mins (Exam Tips review: 10;   Pre-listening: 5–10;
Listening practice 1: 10;   Listening practice 2: 10;
Vocabulary review: 10–15;   Exam listening: 20)

Revision

As this unit includes a round-up and revision of listening activities from previous units, further revision will probably not be appropriate.

Exam Tips review

When checking answers, get students to read out each complete piece of advice, as this will help to reinforce it in their minds, and ask them to explain the reason(s) for the advice. Remind them of any extra points from the Exam Tips.

The main message of all the tips is that thinking about the subject and the task in advance will make the listening process easier.

KEY Exam Tips review

1 D (ET 7, Unit 5)	5 B (ET 14, Unit 9)
2 F (ET 2, Unit 1)	6 G (ET 17, Unit 11)
3 E (ET 5, Unit 3)	7 A (ET 8, Unit 5)
4 C (ET 11, Unit 7)	

Pre-listening

1 Let students look through the (genuine) examples for a few moments and discuss the mistakes together. If someone can't work out an intended meaning, encourage other students to explain it to them.

When checking, encourage students to suggest why the mistakes were made, e.g. pronunciation problems (the student has written the word the way he or she hears or says it): 1, 2, 4; grammar problems (countable/uncountable nouns): 1, 5; grammar problems (passive): 6; vocabulary problems: 2, 3.

2 Keep this discussion fairly short but ask for brief feedback and be prepared to offer practical advice and encouragement if appropriate.

Listening practice 1

Point out that in some exam questions the information is not directly stated but has to be worked out from the evidence in the text. Common examples are when you are asked to describe someone's mood, (*frightened*, *angry* etc.) or behaviour (*helpful*, *unfriendly* etc.).

Let students listen to the recordings twice and then discuss their answers in pairs before checking. Some may find the problem in B more difficult to understand and in this case, explain that as the speaker didn't use the correct word for 'canoe' and the people who hired out canoes didn't understand him, they thought he must be telling them his name!

KEY Listening practice 1

1 A B   2 C D

Tapescript

A   Well, I had quite an amusing time in Greece on one holiday because I confused the words for 'Good morning', which is 'Kalimera', and 'squid', which is 'Kalamari'. So for several days I was going around smiling broadly at people, saying 'squid' to them, and I couldn't understand why they looked at me as if I was totally crazy until someone pointed it out.

B   I was in France on holiday, staying in a friend's cottage and one day we decided to go for a trip on the river. So we went along to a place on the river where you could hire canoes. And a friend, who prided himself on being rather good at speaking French, went in to hire the canoes. We decided we needed three, so he asked for 'trois canneurs' which he thought was the French for 'three canoes'. We got our canoes; we spent the afternoon on the river, we came back. And Stephen went in to return the canoes and collect the deposit he'd paid on them. And as he walked in the door, they said 'Ah, hello Mr Troiscanneurs ...'

C   Once I had an interview with someone called Paddy Russell and I'd never met this person so I went to their office, I knocked on the door – a lady answered the door and I said 'Hello, I've come to see Paddy Russell' and she said, 'Yes.' and I said, 'Is he in?', and she said, 'No, but I am'. I was really embarrassed! And ever since then I've always gone to great lengths to discover what sex people are even if they have names where you can't really tell.

D   One of the things that I found strange when I first went to Australia was the way people there use the expression 'See you later'. They say it all the time. The first few times it happened, I thought they meant it – I remember chatting to an Australian on the way over and as we got off the plane, he said, 'See you later'. I was a bit surprised but I really expected to meet him somewhere later that day. Of course, I didn't. I never saw him again, in fact.

Listening practice 2

As well as providing practice in intensive listening, this information is included to remind students of the practical details of Paper 4, and they may want to ask other questions at this point. The average score for pass candidates may reassure those suffering a crisis of confidence!

Encourage students to predict answers to all the questions in sections 1 and 2 and to hazard guesses where necessary. If you prefer to deal with the two sections separately, you will need to stop the tape after

... There are always four parts to the test ... in order to check answers. (This is marked*.)

Similar information about Paper 5 is included in Unit 16.

KEY Listening practice 2

1 1 True   2 True   3 False   4 False   5 False   6 True
   7 True   8 False (There are always four parts)

2 1 40 minutes   2 30   3 60%   4 40%

Tapescript

OK, let me tell you about what'll happen when you take the Listening test next week. First of all, once you're all sitting down and everything, the supervisor – the person in charge – will switch on the tape recorder and you'll hear some general information. It'll tell you, for example, that you are going to hear each part of the test twice and that you will have time before each part to look through the questions and time after each part to think about your answers.

After that, the supervisor stops the tape recorder and hands out the question papers and the answer sheets. That's the time to ask questions if you have any, or to mention any problems, because you can't speak during the actual test. So if you have a problem hearing the tape recorder, for example, or if your pen has run out, you should say so now. I'd take a spare pen with you if I were you. But don't take any correcting fluid – you know that white stuff you use to correct mistakes – you're not allowed to use that. OK, once you've got your question paper, write your name and your examination index number on it clearly, and sign the answer sheet in the space at the top.

Now when the test begins, make sure you use the time before each part to look through the questions. That's really valuable, as I keep telling you. The question paper has instructions for each part and these are also repeated on the tape. For Part One, you'll hear the questions too, so you can't get lost! You'll probably find it easiest to write your answers on the question paper first, though you don't need to – you can write directly on to the answer sheet if you prefer. At the end, you get five minutes to transfer your answers from the question paper to the answer sheet. Make sure you copy them carefully.

There are always four parts to the test.* It takes about forty minutes in all, though it'll probably seem to go like a flash. There are thirty questions and each question is worth one mark. Cambridge says that on average people who pass First Certificate get about sixty per cent on the Listening – I'm sure you can manage that. Remember that the Listening and the Speaking parts of the exam are important – together they make up forty per cent of the marks for the whole exam. Any questions?

Vocabulary review

1 The words are all connected with topics from previous units. This activity works best if students collaborate. Establish suitable headings for each group of words and use the checking phase to make sure they know precise meanings (e.g. flyover, level crossing) and to check pronunciation (e.g. brooch /brəʊtʃ/ necklace (/nekləs/). You could also revise other words in the same categories.

2 Again the phrasal verbs are drawn from previous exercises. Students may prefer to tackle the task alone initially but it's useful if they compare answers.

KEY   Vocabulary review

1 Photography: film   flash   negative   camera   close-up
Road features: bend   flyover   fork   level crossing   junction
Parts of the body: shoulder   elbow   wrist   ankle   knee
Parts of a house: basement   loft   balcony   chimney   floor
Jewellery: bracelet   ring   brooch   necklace   earring
2 1 off   2 through   3 in   4 out   5 off; back   6 on; up

Exam listening: Crossed lines

Introduce the topic by explaining what a *crossed line* is and finding out if anyone has had the experience of hearing another conversation going on while they were speaking to someone on the telephone.

Let students read through the instructions carefully and check that they understand exactly what they're going to hear and what they have to do. Point out particularly that they will hear the beginning of a call before the crossed line which they need to identify.

1 It may be helpful to stop after the first extract and check that everyone has identified the correct extension. Check answers before playing the recording again for the Exam task.

2 Allow students time to compare answers and to discuss any differences. When checking answers, make sure the reasons why the right answer is right and the others are wrong are clearly established (it is often very helpful to quote from the tapescript here).

KEY   Exam listening: Crossed lines

1 1 3   2 5   3 2   4 9   5 7   6 1

2 1 B   (The person who took the booking must have forgotten to write it down.)

2 C   (We're trying our best to get it repaired...)

3 B   (What do you call it?)

4 D   (two chambermaids... My hotel is very short-staffed...)

5 A   (Haven't you got any trained staff to supervise things and advise people properly?)

6 D   (Can you get someone to bring my luggage down?)

7 A   (Tell him he'll have a real problem)

Tapescript

1 a: Train Enquiries. Can I help you?
b: Hello, Could you tell me the times of the trains to...

A: I don't believe this! What do you mean you haven't got a table? I made the booking over a week ago!

a: This is Train Enquiries...
b: I'm sorry. We seem to have a crossed line. (*a hangs up*)

B: ... I understand how you feel, sir, but there simply isn't any room. The person who took your booking must have forgotten to write it down. I'm afraid it was just a mistake. He's new, you see.

A: Just a mistake! Do you realise I've invited some very important people to dine with me tonight? That mistake could cost me an important contract!

B: I'm sorry, sir. I suggest you phone your colleagues and explain the problem. I'm sure you'll find somewhere else to entertain them. I can recommend several other very good places to eat round here...

A: I can't contact them now. One's probably on his way from New York at this very minute! Surely you could fit one more table in?

B: Not unless you'd like me to put it in the corridor, sir.

A: Well, you haven't heard the last of this I can tell you...

2 a: Theatre Royal
b: I'd like to book two tickets for...

A: A striped shirt, I said. I was told it would be ready by 4 o'clock and it's already 4.20.

a: Two tickets for what?
b: I'm sorry. It's a crossed line. I'll try and ring back. (*a rings off*)

B: ... you see we've had a bit of a problem with our pressing equipment. We're a bit behind.
A: Well, I'm due to leave in half an hour, and I need that shirt now!
B: I'm sorry. As I've explained, we've had a bit of a problem.
A: Well, let me have as it is. I'll wear it unpressed. It probably won't show too much under a jacket.
B: I'm afraid you won't be able to wear it as it is. We're trying our best to get it repaired for you at the moment...

3 a: 771649.
b: Hello, I'm interested in your advertisement for...

A: Two lime sodas.

b: Oh no. (*rings off*)

B: Yes and ...what do you call it?
A: I don't know sir.
B: Yes, you know, one of those pancake things.
A: Sweet or savoury sir?
B: Savoury. Oh, you know – they're Chinese.
A: A pancake roll.
B: Two.
A: Two pancake rolls Anything else sir?
B: Yes, that's only for starters...

4 a: Red and White Taxis
b: I'd like a taxi as soon as possible.
a: Where to?

A: ... two chambermaids.

a: I'm sorry. Where to?
b: Oh this is hopeless! (*a rings off*)

B: ...and when do you want them to start?
A: Well, as soon as possible, really. My hotel is very short-staffed at the moment. Some of the guests have started complaining...
B: You realise that you'll have to pay double time over the holiday period?
A: Double time? Are you sure? I don't usually pay special rates.
B: Maybe that's why you're short-staffed, sir. So, double time and you supply the uniform. Free meals, of course, and a taxi to get them home in the evening...
A: This is outrageous! Do you think I'm made of money?
B: They're the normal conditions, sir, and if you want extra staff at short notice...

5 a: Reception. How can I help you?
  b: This is Room 509. Look I'm still getting crossed lines every time I try to
    make a call. It's just not good enough…

  A: … and I can hardly move at all this morning…

  a: Sorry, madam?
  b: It's just another crossed line!
  a: I'll speak to the engineer. (*Rings off hurriedly*)

  B: … I'm sorry to hear that, sir.
  A: I wasn't warned that this might happen. Ah, I mean, I'm in agony.
  B: Well, you use the equipment at your own risk. It says so in the brochure you
    were given.
  A: That's not the point. Haven't you got any trained staff to supervise things
    and advise people properly?
  B: Well, we have, but I think Debbie must have been on her tea break while
    you were on the exercise bike.
  A: Disgraceful!
  B: But if you only did five minutes pedalling, as you say, you shouldn't be
    suffering too much!

6 a: Swindon 761593.
  b: Hello darling, it's me.

  A: Fine, we'll have the bill ready when you come down.

  a: Who's that?
  b: Oh, it's a crossed lined again. I don't believe it! (*a rings off*)

  B: Can you get someone to bring my luggage down?
  A: I'm afraid there's no-one available at the moment. Could you possibly
    manage them on your own?
  B: On my own! Are you serious? They're very heavy. I thought this was a three
    star hotel! There must be somebody there who can help. What about you?
  A: Me? Oh, I can't leave the desk, madam. The only other person here is the
    manager and he's tied up with a problem…
  B: Tell him he'll have a real problem on his hands if I miss my train because of
    this hotel's incompetence.
  A: I'll see what I can do…

Unit 16 **Speaking review**

Timing guide

50–70 mins (Exam Tips review: 5–10;   Pictures: 10;
Language practice: 15–20;   Pronunciation: 10–15;   Task 1: 5–10;
Task 2:   10–15)

Revision

As this unit includes a round-up of various aspects of speaking practice
from previous units, additional revision may not be appropriate.

Exam Tips review

It's a good idea to let students read and discuss these together. When
checking answers, make sure students can explain reasons for their
answers, and be prepared to remind them of additional points.

KEY   Exam Tips review

1 True: don't waste a lot of time worrying about what to say. The
   sooner you start, the more language the examiner will hear from
   you. You've only got about a minute, after all. (ET 22, Unit 14)
2 True: answer as fully as possible. (ET 3 and 4, Unit 2)
3 False: and the examiner will be impressed if you use an appropriate
   expression to ask for clarification. (ET 13, Unit 8)
4 True: you'll be marked on 'using a wide range of vocabulary'.
   (ET 10, Unit 6)
5 False: in the second and third parts of the test, you should talk to
   your partner. (Foundation unit)
6 False: use words you do know to express the meaning. (ET 9, Unit 6)
7 False: the language you use to talk about the problem is just as
   important. (ET 13, Unit 8)
8 False: pronunciation represents two of the six categories you'll be
   marked on. (Foundation unit)

Pictures

Remind students about the basic procedure for talking about a
photograph, suggested in Exam Tip 22 (Unit 14), if they have found this
helpful.

Monitor students' work, assessing how successful their learning has
been and make notes of any emergency repair work necessary!

Language practice: Consequences

This exercise should be a quick, fun revision of the first conditional, focusing on intonation and stress in longer utterances.

KEY   Language practice: Consequences

1 C   2 D   3 B   4 A   5 F   6 E

At the end, if time allows, invite students to add their own ideas to the list of situations for each other to respond to.

Tapescript

1 If you go to the disco, you'll probably have a great time.
2 If you really enjoy yourself, you certainly won't want to leave early.
3 If you leave too late, you'll miss the last bus.
4 If you miss the bus, you may not be able find a taxi.
5 If you have to walk, you won't get home till dawn.
6 If you don't get any sleep tonight, you'll fall asleep in class tomorrow.

Pronunciation 1: Revision of sounds

1 Encourage students to remember the sounds represented by the symbols. You could help by giving definitions of words containing the sounds which they have practised before: e.g. *cat/bat*; *hard/calm*.

2 Here the words in the list should help students to remember the sounds. If not, they should look at the reference list on page 104.

KEY   **Pronunciation 1:** Revision of sounds

1 friend, pet, next, petrol;
practise, exam, cat, flats;
father, classmate, party, garden.

2 *Group 1* tough   gloves   jumper
Group 2 cough   collar   wallet
Group 3 through   suit   shoe
Group 4 thought   warm   talk
Group 5 although   coat   brooch

Tapescript

Group 1   tough   gloves   jumper
Group 2   cough   collar   wallet
Group 3   through   suit   shoe
Group 4   thought   warm   talk
Group 5   although   coat   brooch

Pronunciation 2: Revision of word stress

If students don't grasp the system of using large and small boxes to represent stressed and unstressed syllables, give more examples and ask them to draw boxes for a few words e.g. donkey, □□ butterfly □□□.

KEY   **Pronunciation 2:** Revision of word stress

1 □□ forecast   practise
2 □□ compare   control
3 □□□ exhausted   delighted
4 □□□ telephone   interested

5 □□□□ photography
      advertisement
6 □□□ introduce   guarantee

Tapescript

1 forecast   practise
2 compare   control
3 exhausted   delighted
4 telephone   interested
5 photography   advertisement
6 introduce   guarantee

Tasks

Try to make this as realistic as possible. Check that students know what to do for both 1 and 2, but don't explain any words they may not know. Reassure them that this will be done later, if necessary. (This gives them a chance to use discourse strategies as appropriate.)

Tell them that they have no more than five minutes for Task 1 and the same for Task 2, and monitor them to make sure that no student spends more than about a minute talking about 'their' pair of pictures.

Note any good uses of language as they work and sum up at the end, as positively as possible, giving examples of good usage you have noted.

KEY   **Check your Speaking test facts**

1 b) 14–16
2 b) 20%
3 a) 60%

Unit 17 Practice test: Listening

This unit is designed to be used as a 'mock' test for Paper 4. As in the exam, all the instructions are given on the tape and each passage should be played twice. The timings given below are based on this approach.

If possible, give students the opportunity to do this in one continuous sitting, so that they can get the feel of how the real exam will be. They will almost certainly be surprised at how quickly it passes. If time allows, let them mark their own tests by giving them the answers and re-playing the tape, stopping to discuss any problems as they arise.

Timing guide

30 mins (Part one: 7; Part two: 8; Part three: 7; Part four: 8)

KEY   (1 mark each)

Part one
1 A   2 B   3 C   4 B   5 B   6 A   7 C   8 C

Part two
9 TV series   10 wildlife/animals   11 engines   12 ambulances
13 fly (the plane)   14 challenges   15 captain of a ship
16 heart attack   17 car headlights   18 the next/following
    morning/day

Part three
19 E   20 A   21 B   22 D   23 C

Part four
24 C   25 A   26 B   27 B   28 C   29 A   30 C

Part one

You will hear people talking in eight different situations. For questions 1–8, choose the best answer A, B or C.

pause

tone

Woman:	I've known him about six months now, and we get on well, so I was really looking forward to meeting these friends of his. He was always talking about how crazy they were, so I thought it would be a real laugh. But they turned out to be quite ordinary. And we didn't have that much to say to each other – I felt a bit fed up really, it wasn't his fault, just that I'd expected too much I suppose.

pause

tone (The piece is repeated.)

Man: How would you like to find out about a very special promotion we're running in this area for the coming month? You don't have to do anything at all – you don't have to sign anything or go anywhere – we aren't pushing bargain prices or free gifts. We just want you to have the chance to find out about our brilliant new range of designer fitted kitchen units, with no obligation at all. All you have to do is agree to receive our video through the post. It's absolutely free.

pause

tone (The piece is repeated.)

Woman: This is quite interesting, really, because they've brought together a number of people from different parts of the music world...

Man: Yeah, but that's been happening more and more recently. What we haven't had before, to my knowledge at least, is people looking at a whole variety of different musical sources and saying, like, 'I can sing that' wherever it comes from.

Woman: Oh, yes. I agree. The range of numbers you get on the album, jazz, opera, folk, pop – it's great.

pause

tone (The piece is repeated.)

Man: It's my first time helping to finalise a deal, and I've had it all week about what a lot of business this firm gives us, they're one of our biggest clients, etcetera. So I've got to watch what I say, let Mike do the talking, because he's the boss and I'm only a junior salesman.

Woman: Yeah.

Man: So, fine – in spite of the train strike, I get there dead on time, but I just sit quietly like I was told, and they're waiting around, and Mike comes strolling in after half an hour and says, have I got it all sorted? Have I got it all sorted! I felt a real fool.

pause

tone (The piece is repeated.)

Receptionist: Yes, what can we do for you?

Woman: I've just seen the nurse and she said I've got to come back in two weeks so she can check my arm's healing properly, and everything...

Receptionist: Right, so you'd like an appointment...

Woman: But they also need the doctor to do some tests before they can finish with me, you see, so, um, can I make an appointment for the nurse at the end of the week after next, okay, and for the doctor, um, about a week before that?

pause

tone (The piece is repeated.)

Boy: She's okay, better than most, I suppose. She gives me a bit of money when she can. It isn't much, but it covers most of my clothes and if I go out with my friends some nights. And I've got a weekend job as a waiter too, so that helps. But she's always on at me to eat more, she makes all this stuff and then gets mad when I won't have it. But the thing is, I've got to stay fit, 'cause I'm in training, I can't afford to carry any extra weight.

pause

tone (The piece is repeated.)

Woman: There is one point which I feel I must make about this particular book though, especially after all the publicity it's had. I don't think anyone could question the amount of research Bernard put into his work. But he has, in fact, given us an extremely dull read, and that's got to be a problem no matter how many attractive illustrations there are. It's such a pity, because just a bit more work from a good editor would have made all the difference. Wouldn't you agree?

pause

tone (The piece is repeated.)

Woman: We regret to announce a delay in flight BA 112 to Manchester. Passengers who have onward connecting flights from Manchester to other destinations should go immediately to the British Airways Information Desk on the ground floor where staff will be pleased to assist. All other passengers are requested to remain in the Departure Lounge on the first floor and await further announcements. Refreshments will be available from the Coffee Shop on production of a boarding pass. We apologise for the delay which is due to technical problems.

pause

tone (The piece is repeated.)

That is the end of Part one.

Part two

You will hear part of a radio programme about the Royal Flying Doctor Service of Australia. For questions 9–18, complete the sentences.

pause

tone

There's three main areas of the service's work: aviation, medicine and communication. Aviation: we started off with canvas covered bi-planes, we now have pressurised prop-jets. The 'Nomad' that some people will see in the TV series 'The Flying Doctor' is still used but they're being phased out – they're at the end of their useful life. Planes in the service unfortunately have a very, very hard life. They're landing and taking off quite often on dirt strips; they have collisions with wild life from time to time; the red dust that is all through the outback gets into engines and instrumentation and can make an awful mess!

Our planes, though, are as well-equipped as any intensive care ambulance in any big city in the world. They have humidicribs, they have full life-support gear. You name it, it's in these planes. Our planes are flown by qualified experienced commercial pilots – our doctors do not fly themselves, because the doctor obviously could be giving someone cardiac massage or helping in the delivery of a baby – they can't also be flying a plane.

And we keep our pilots and often have pilots applying to fly with the service simply because flying with the service provides all sorts of challenges that pilots don't have to meet on their their normal commercial runs. They have sole responsibility of deciding in an emergency whether or not a plane will fly, much like the captain of a ship. The, an emergency call may come in but it's up to the pilot to decide whether or not the flight can be made.

We had an instance recently out of Broken Hill where a call came in from a tiny, tiny little place called Pack Saddle which is half way between Broken Hill and Tibooburra, in the middle of nowhere, and a tourist out there who was having a heart attack – could the doctor come out? It was the middle of the night and there was a raging storm. The pilot thought about it and said, 'No, can't fly at night under those conditions because Pack Saddle doesn't have electrified lighting for its airstrip.' Now under certain conditions we can use people in their cars with their headlights on the strip to light the strip or we fill metal drums with dirt and sump oil and light that, to light the strip, but that can only be under fairly good conditions. So the pilot said no. He actually flew out and picked up the patient the next morning. The patient subsequently died but his widow is actually trying to raise the money to electrify the strip at Pack Saddle. So we have very experienced pilots and they very much enjoy their work. On to medicine...

pause

tone

Now you will hear Part two again. (The piece is repeated.)

pause

That is the end of Part two.

Part three

You will hear five different people talking about cities. For questions 19–23, choose from the list A–F which place is being described. Write the letter next to the number.

pause

tone

...and unfortunately there have been quite a lot of people saying it's not very nice, especially in the centre, and my parents were getting a bit worried and Dad started going on about choosing somewhere nearer home, but I'm sure it'll be fine and I'll be in a hostel and make friends as soon as my course starts. And the night life is supposed to be pretty cool, but don't tell my Mum I said that.

…but honestly, I mean when you hear people talk about it now you'd think it was a really terrible place, but we didn't think so. We had lots of aunties and uncles all living in the same neighbourhood and everyone was in and out of each other's houses all day long. My father used to complain about working conditions, but none of us ever thought it was a bad place for a family to live. The thought didn't occur to us.

…and of course it's all extremely well cared for with lovely parks and roadside cafés and lots of pedestrianised shopping areas and everything, though not much character, if you know what I mean. I took my mother and my aunt and they had a fantastic fortnight. And I must admit I did too. But it's a bit unreal, somehow. I couldn't imagine settling down there and going out to an ordinary office job every day. I'm sure your parents would love it, though.

…so although we hadn't seen it ourselves, we'd listened to the grown-ups' stories and always had rather a romantic image of it. My brother and I used to make up adventures, like, what we'd do if we could ever go there. And I'd like to some day. I think it's got lots of interesting architecture and stuff, apart from the historical connection with my family. Course it's only very recently that anyone can travel there, because of the political situation. I know my mum wouldn't've wanted to – too many bad memories – but I might one day.

…only there for a year and it's just too good a chance to miss. I've got a really good deal on the flights, because of booking so early, 'cause of course it gets very expensive in the season, and my accommodation will be free, I can sleep on their floor, I've known them since we were at college. And I'll see all those incredible old buildings and ruins you're always reading about in the magazines.

pause

tone

Now you will hear Part three again. (The piece is repeated.)

pause

That is the end of Part three.

Part four

You will hear a taxi driver talking about his job. For questions 24–30, choose the best answer A, B or C.

pause

tone

Interviewer: What is it that you enjoy about driving a taxi, Chris?

Taxi Driver: Well, I mean you do it for money, obviously, like most jobs. But I enjoy the um, I suppose I enjoy being my own boss, you know, doing what I want to do. And you're very much in control of of what you do, you decide what area you're going to do, when to have a break, stuff like that. One thing you have to be always thinking about is where you might pick up a passenger. Will the opera house be turning out? Do they have an afternoon performance? What time will the planes be coming in? I wonder if there are any trains arriving. You're always sort of…scheming to make an extra bit of money. And the relationship between reward and effort is very immediate. Um you, you make the right decisions, you get a fare and they pay you, (excuse me) you know. You don't have to wait till the end of the month! You meet, well you meet some people who aren't all that nice, but the vast majority of people are very nice. If you're pleased to talk to them, they're mostly pleased to talk to you. You get a feel for people who don't want to talk to you, obviously the first couple of one word answers will tell you…

Interviewer:	So you always start talking?
Taxi Driver:	I always wish people 'Good morning' or Good afternoon' or whatever, 'How are you?' which gets things off to a good start. Because quite a few people have a general dislike of taxi drivers.
Interviewer:	Do they?
Taxi Driver:	Well, they do. I mean, the mere fact they can't get a cab the minute they want one makes them annoyed, you know, and if the cab takes half an hour or so to come, you know, people are beside themselves! 'Why is it so?', you know, 'Why didn't you come sooner?' 'Well, I was on the other side of town at the time, sir!', you know. But, um start them off well, on a sunny day, people are pleasant, happy. You meet some people who are famous.
Interviewer:	Like?
Taxi Driver:	Well, I took Louisa Wallis to the airport on Sunday, who's…famous, from soap operas, a big soap opera star in, um what was it? 'Fathers and Sons' – oh you must have seen it. She played Gertie for years. Oh yes, yes, famous, well-known. And I took Brian Best, the sports commentator, to a football match a little while ago. (*Laughs*) He told me a few good jokes, I remember.
Interviewer:	Have you ever made a friend of somebody you took in your cab?
Taxi Driver:	No. No, I haven't actually. I suppose they're brief encounters that aren't really suitable to be extended. There's a certain professional distance, I suppose. There's a line beyond which I don't feel that I, I want to go. I don't want to make friends of everybody in the world. I just happen to like having a little chat with them for a while. I suppose I was born for that sort of thing. I'd have made a good shop assistant. I'd have made a lovely menswear assistant, something like that. Very nice, charming and friendly but don't need to talk at any length.

pause

tone

Now you will hear Part four again. (The piece is repeated.)

pause

That is the end of the test.

Unit 18 **Practice test: Speaking**

This unit is designed to be a 'mock' test for Paper 5, so that students can get a clear picture of how the test is structured. The unit is organised so that all of the test may be done as pairwork, but it is also possible for Part One (talking about yourself) and Part Four (discussion) to be done with the whole class, if you prefer.

It is also possible, if you can find time, to conduct the whole test for each pair yourself. In this case, the students need only look at the pictures for Part Two and the list of suggestions for Part Three, while you use the questions in the Student's Book.

Whichever way your class uses this practice test, try to ensure that the timing is adhered to, so that candidates can feel how the time passes. They are usually surprised how short it is.

Before beginning, it may be useful to run through the structure of the Speaking test, reminding students how it develops from personal exchanges (about three minutes), to individual long turns with pictures (about four minutes), to the collaborative task (about three minutes) leading into discussion (about four minutes). Point out that these times cover both candidates and all the instructions, so the actual time they have to speak is probably little more than five minutes each in total. It is important that they use their time to show what they can do – keeping quiet won't earn any marks.

You may wish to revise the different parts of the Speaking test with the students before they do their 'mock', or suggest that they look back through the Speaking units themselves.

Part One – Unit 10, Unit 12
Part Two – Unit 2, Unit 6, Unit 14, Unit 16
Part Three – Unit 4, Unit 8, Unit 12, Unit 14, Unit 16
Part Four – Unit 14, Unit 16

Index of speaking and listening skills

Listening skills